SCOTLAND'S

HIDDEN

SACRED

PAST

Teddy Silva

Also by this Author

The Missing Lands:
Uncovering Earth's Pre-flood Civilization

First Templar Nation: How the Knights Templar
Created Europe's First Nation-state

The Lost Art of Resurrection: Initiation, Secret Chambers
and the Quest for the Otherworld

The Divine Blueprint: Temples, Power Places and
the Global Plan to Shape the Human Soul
(formerly 'Common Wealth')

Secrets In The Fields:
The Science and Mysticism of Crop Circles

Chartres Cathedral: The Missing or Heretic Guide

Book design by Freddy Silva.

INVISIBLE TEMPLE
www.invisibletemple.com

10 9 8 7 6 5 4 3 2 1

Printed in New England.

It's not about a conclusion.
It's about the way people got there.

- Peter Boghossian

Ring of Brodgar, 1808

CREDITS

Without the invaluable assistance of Maral Nersessian, Researcher at the Institute of History of the National Academy of Sciences of the Republic of Armenia, this work would be lacking in the area of Armenian language and its idiosyncracies. I am also indebted to the late Laurence Gardner for his invaluable research into the lineage of the Tuadhe d'Anu; to John Barber for his generous permission to use his images of Scottish mounds; to the librarians of many universities and libraries for their patience and willingness; Dawn Bramadat and Marilee Marrinan for casting watchful eyes over the text.

No masks were harmed during the writing of this book.

CONTENTS

SHETLAND

ORKNEY
ISLANDS

LEWIS

OUTER HEBRIDES

SCOTLAND

MULL

JURA

ARRAN

EIRE

IRISH SEA

WALES

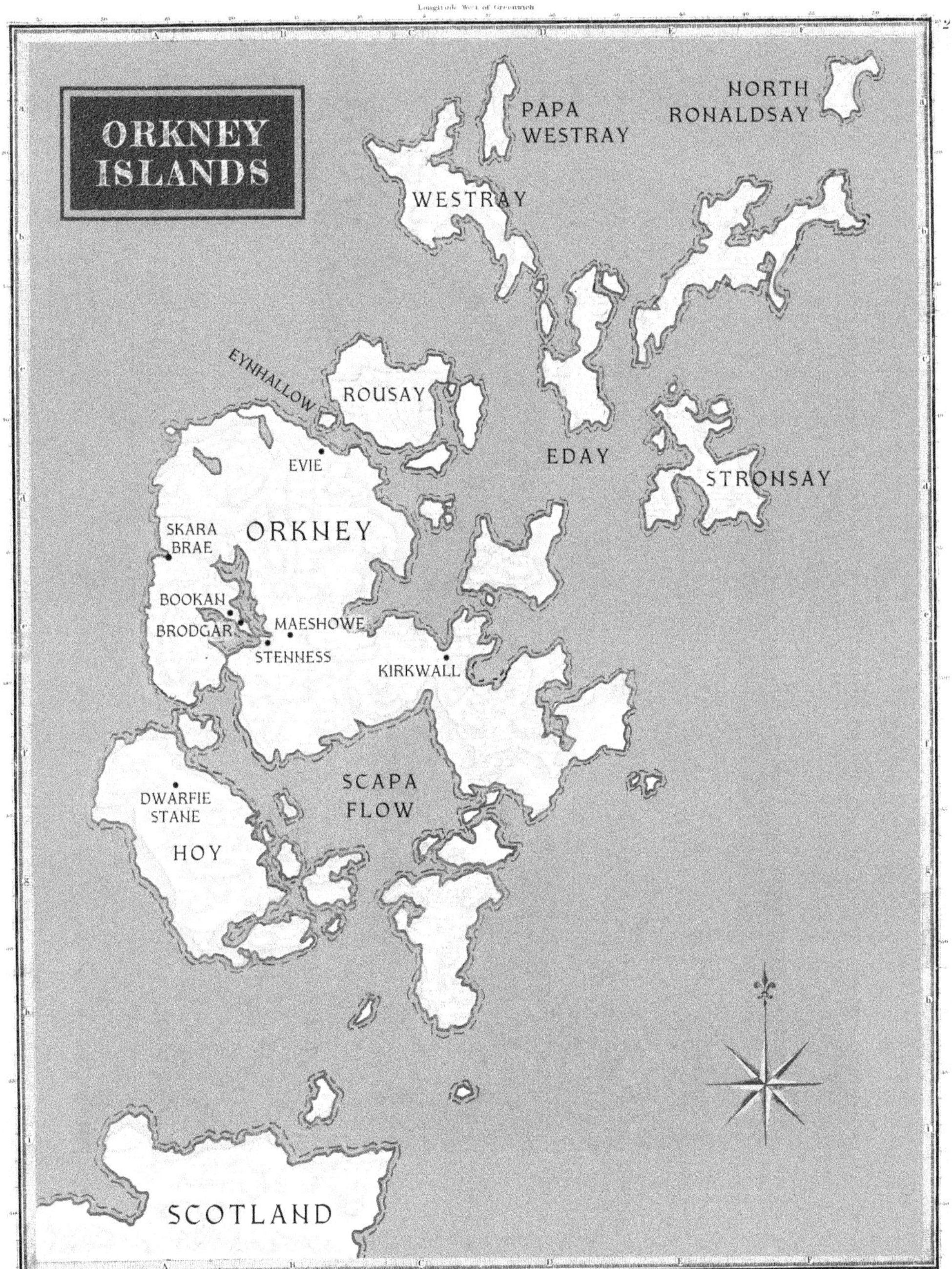

ORKNEY
ISLANDS

Longitude West of Greenwich

PAPA
WESTRAY

NORTH
RONALDSAY

WESTRAY

EYNHALLOW

ROUSAY

EVIE

EDAY

STRONSAY

SKARA
BRAE

ORKNEY

BOOKAN

MAESHOWE

BRODGAR

STENNESS

KIRKWALL

DWARFIE
STANE

SCAPA
FLOW

HOY

SCOTLAND

The stones of Stenness.

1

STONES AT THE END
OF THE WORLD

eyond the northern shore of Scotland lies a narrow waterway with the ominous status of having one of the strongest tides in the world, which, coupled with gale force winds, give rise to some of the most violent sea conditions to be found anywhere. Only those on a mission to outwit the elements attempt to navigate this eight-mile-wide aquatic hell. And yet, despite the odds, someone in the remote past did exactly that. The reward was the archipelago of Orkney, where, at the intersection of lochs Stenness and Harray, a group of unnamed architects erected a machine made of stone.

The circle of Stenness.

When an expedition organized by the naturalist Joseph Banks visited Stenness in 1772, facts about the monument were as sparse as Orkney's trees. His accompanying illustrator, Jonathan Cleveley, memorialized the site in a watercolor that shows only four remaining uprights, along with two outliers and a further ring of stones beyond a narrow bridge. A later traveler mentions a fifth half-broken stone and the remains of a structure in the middle, apparently created from other broken monoliths.[1] All in all it is estimated that eleven of the tallest monoliths in Britain once stood here.[2]

Time, weather, religion, ignorance, necessity and stupidity have all paid visits to the stones of Stenness, leaving only three-and-a-half standing monoliths, and still, incomplete and imperfect, the site spellbinds the casual visitor with magnetic charm, an aura so intact it still projects power without the need of further visual accoutrement. On my first visit I returned no less than five times, the last one nearly causing me to miss my flight home. I have experienced hundreds of such temples around the world, yet even in its state of dilapidation Stenness seduces to the point of addiction.

The predominantly blue-grey calcareous sandstones are peppered with mica and stained red from iron oxide. To watch the sunlight tease the color out of the vertical slabs is to be in the presence of the work of a machinist who moonlighted as a cosmic artist. Or is it the other way around? The comeliest stone stands 19 feet tall, 4 feet wide and barely 8 inches thick. Like the others it rests on its center of gravity, mounted in a shallow socket and chocked with small stones and gravel as though someone foresaw the vigorous winds that are now commonplace across Orkney, the rude intrusion of climate change at these high latitudes. The architect of Stenness clearly ensured the project would defy the elements and survive for future generations to ponder. During excavations in 1906 some of the sockets were found packed with concrete, suggesting the stones had been toppled at some point and respectfully re-erected in their original positions.

One monolith – romantically dubbed Stone 7 – is crooked like a bent nail and visually at odds with the others, like a drunk reveler who arrives at the wrong party. Uncovered and placed upright in 1906, it was described as an "ill-shaped stone...we have doubts as to whether it is a genuine monolith. It looks such a dwarf amid these huge monoliths." Archaeologists considered this black sheep to be the broken part of a much larger stone, added later to compensate for an original that was destroyed.[3]

The circle of Stenness is framed within a massive, slightly elliptical henge, 91 by 105 feet, with an inner ditch cut seven feet deep and thirteen wide into a lone, giant slab of horizontally bedded flagstone, then arduously leveled flat. Subjected to prolonged waterlogging, its course is broken only once by a causeway leading to an even larger collection of stones a mile away.

In the center lies a rectangular stone-lined hearth used for cooking and feasting. It appears the enclosure was reused, as monuments with long life spans tend to be, by people who arrived much later and wished to preserve some connection with the original sacred space. Or they merely appropriated it for practical purposes because no one by then recalled its original function. The hearth contained cremated animal bones, radiocarbon-dated to 3040 BC,[4] while the remains of a few timber post-holes provided dates between 3100-2775 BC,[5] yet none of this proves when the stone circle itself was originally constructed.

Cleveley's watercolor, 1772.

Four hundred feet to the north-northwest, beside a narrow bridge and barely above sea level, rises another thin, 19 foot-tall slab named the Watch Stone; thirty feet to the southwest lies the stump of its forgotten twin. Like similar standing stones from Brittany to Britain, they are said to enjoy going for a walk at night, and these two were no exception: on New Year's Day they were believed "to wrench themselves out of their places and roll down the slope to the sea. There having dipped themselves, they return and resume their accustomed position."[6]

The environs of Stenness are mostly open farmland now, but the 18th century traveling churchman Richard Pococke offers a reliable picture of a much more complex landscape: "There are two standing stones to the south, one is wanting, and then there are two standing to the West, a third lying down, then two are wanting, there being a space of 27 yards so that there were eight in all. Eighteen yards south east from the Circle is a single stone, and 125 yards to the east of that is another with a hole in it on one side towards the bottom from which going to-wards the circle

Stenness and its outliers, 1805.

is another 73 yards from the fossee, the outer part of which fossee is 16 yards from the Circle."[7]

The stone "with a hole in it" was a celebrated monolith known locally as the Odin Stone, and it once stood on a slight mound by the edge of the peninsula. It played a crucial role in sealing agreements and binding marriages. Vows were made absolute by clasping hands through the hole and swearing an unbreakable pact known as the Odin Oath, considered sacred and as binding as a marriage. Up into the 18th century it was custom for a courting couple to steal away to Stenness, where the woman, in the presence of her lover, would kneel down and pray to Odin to enable her to perform her obligations; the couple then walked along the promontory and up to a second stone circle, where the man pronounced the same request. Together they returned to the Odin Stone and, taking each other's hand through the stone, made a commitment to be constant and faithful to each other. People went to extremes before breaking their vows, as the Reverend Henry illustrates in 1784: "This ceremony was held so very sacred in those times that the person who dared to break the engagement made here was counted infamous, and excluded from all society."[8]

One such case involved a young man who had seduced a girl under promise of marriage. The girl fell pregnant and was subsequently deserted, prompting the man to be brought before a court: "The young man was called before session; the elders were particularly severe. Being asked by the minister the cause of so much rigour, they answered: 'You do not know what a bad man this is; he has broke the promise of Odin.' Being further asked what they meant by the promise of Odin, they put him in mind of the stone at Stenness, with the round hole in it; and added, that it was customary, when promises were made, for the contracting parties to join hands through this hole, and the promises so made were called the promises of Odin." [9] The binding power of the stone even applied to pirates such as John Gow, who, while in Stromness, fell in love with a Miss Gordon, daughter of a local merchant. Keeping with tradition Miss Gordon took Gow to the Odin Stone. A few months later Gow was captured off Eday and summarily executed in London. Distraught at the death of her lover, Miss Gordon is said to have traveled to London in order to touch the hand of Gow's corpse to release herself from the oath.

The stone was also believed to have curative properties. In 1903 it was said that "a child passed through the hole when young would never shake with palsy in old age. Up to the time of its destruction, it was customary to leave some offering on visiting the stone, such as a piece of bread, or cheese, or a rag, or even a stone." [10] Certainly there was an enduring association between the properties of the megalith and magic that endured into modern times. One account describes how walking around the stone nine times during full moons and peering through the hole enabled one to see a mystical island in the sea that was normally not visible to mortals.

But this Utopian idyll came tumbling earthwards in December 1814 when the Odin Stone was broken up by incoming tenant farmer Captain John MacKay who, pleased with his act of wanton vandalism, grabbed a drill and a bag of gunpowder and set his sights on Stenness itself. Word was sent out to Sheriff Peterkin – interrupting his Christmas dinner – who rode out to

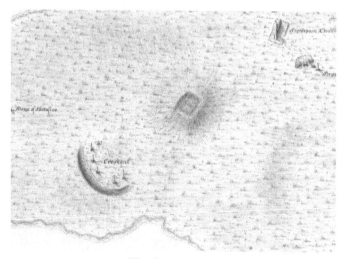

The lost mound.

Stenness, only to find three of its stones already "torn from the spot on which they had stood for ages, and...shivered to pieces." When villagers discovered their beloved temple laid to rubble, their wrath came down on MacKay like divine brimstone. As the landlord had evicted tenants from the farm prior to the arrival of MacKay the Ferry Louper (local slang for a non-resident), ill will was already running high. His cynical use of the stones as a quarry for building material was the last straw. Outraged villagers attempted twice to set fire to MacKay's house, and from that point forward, the misguided Captain's peace was truncated for years to come.

The section of the Odin Stone containing the hole was later found by the horse-mill at the farm, sunk into the ground to anchor external gear wheels.

But there's one other important component missing at Stenness. Frederick Walden, a naval architect and surveyor, made a systematic survey of Orkney as part of Bank's expedition of 1772. On one of his maps, a rectangular mound rises prominently between the stone circle and the church to the east, afterward ploughed away as the land came under increasing pressure from agricultural development. No mention of the mound has surfaced since, which is odd because this was no ordinary mound. While looking through the expedition's illustrations, I came across a drawing by John Frederick Miller, one of the

Miller's missing quadrangle.

draughtsmen accompanying Banks, of a monument that has escaped everyone's attention. In the foreground, a man sits on a broken stone drawing two megaliths, one leaning on the other, while a further six stones as tall as Stenness stand behind him. There's no mistaking the position and orientation of the illustrator, he is on high ground, with Stenness itself, now merely a semi-circle, positioned in the background with the loch beyond.

Between the watercolor and the survey one is given the impression of a quadrangular stone monument, and if so, the design would be consistent with similar enclosures such as Crucuno in Carnac, Avebury in England, and Xerez in Portugal, all of which were designed to calculate the extreme rising and setting of the Sun and Moon.[11]

The big question now remains: who in their right minds sailed to the ends of the Earth to erect this impressive collection of monuments?

Certainly they were a cut above your average Neolithic knuckle-dragger. The design of the circle of Stenness alone is unique among its peers. Each flat-faced monolith resembles a tablet with tip deliberately cut and angled – one at 40°, angle of the nonagon, esoteric symbol of utmost perfection, another at 51°, the angle of slope of the Great Pyramid – each pointing assertively at the sky for reasons that remain as obscure as the origin of its creator. If one were to imagine the circle reconstructed, Stenness would resemble a modern-looking meeting place for a high council, a ring for the conduct of academic inquiry, or a parliament (it was still remembered as such in the 19th century).[12] And while stone circles generally tend to be devices for measuring the motions of the sky, the aura projected by Stenness is different, it is one of uprightness and debate.

This was the impression I was left with, as were the first Scandinavian settlers, who recorded local memories of a group of distinguished people wearing white robes who were intimately associated with this and other Orkney temples long ago.[13] The only certainty is that Stenness is the oldest monument on the archipelago, part of a 370 square-mile enterprise comprising 80 known megalithic passage mounds, 250 round barrows, 100 short cists, stone-lined graves and earthen burial sites. Many more now lie underwater courtesy of an ocean on the rise.

Stenness is the *axis mundi* of Neolithic Orkney.

But who was brave enough to journey here thousands of years ago and create a remote civilization at the very edge of the northern world?

The Ring of Brodgar.

LAND OF ORCS

rkney is best described as remnants of a plateau dissected into eighty islands by rising seas following the demise of the Ice Age into what now resembles a jigsaw. The exception is the island of Hoy, an omnipresent and barren mountain composed almost entirely of moorland.

At this northern latitude the winter Sun scribes a thin arc above the horizon, its orb rising a mere 8° over the low hills to provide no more than six hours of sunlight. This is compensated for in summer with eighteen hours of light, so when insomnia drives you to read a book at 1 AM, you can do so outdoors until you fall asleep, only to be roused by the Sun rising two hours later.

Around 16,000 BC Scotland lay below a mile-thick sheet of ice, at which point Orkney was a large island encircling a wide bay and barely connected to the mainland. Then the climate began to warm, allowing species such as mammoth, woolly rhinoceros and reindeer to move north. Their tenure was brief, wiped out by the great flood of 9703 BC (otherwise known as the Younger Dryas boundary), which deposited a layer of sand across the region. The ensuing rise in sea level transformed Orkney into two islands, and two thousand years later, a low-lying archipelago.[1]

Incredible as it may seem, people were calling this seemingly freezing and inhospitable region home in 11,000 BC, as proven by the discovery of flint scrapers in sedimentary core samples taken from the ocean floor at a depth of 450 feet between Orkney and the Shetland Islands to the north.[2] An alarming picture of a rapidly changing Earth is painted, with survivors forced to adapt to an unstable climate. Another cache of flints was found on the island of Stronsay dating to 9000 BC, demonstrating that humans were living here tenaciously after the flood and well before the rest of Scotland was inhabited.[3]

It turns out that the end of the Younger Dryas was a blessing for Orkney. Bathed by the warm waters of the Gulf Stream it remained relatively free of ice and enjoyed a comparatively warm climate, so much so that it was able to accommodate refugees from the rising North Atlantic Ocean, specifically from the Shetlands. Evidence of human habitation on Orkney itself dates to 6660 BC,[4] but whoever the inhabitants were and whatever they might have built was convincingly wiped out by a 15 to 30-foot wall of water, a mega-tsunami caused by an underwater slide off the coast of Norway c.6200 BC.[5]

Once again, life persevered. Around 5000 BC the land was covered in birch-hazel woodland, yet within 1200 years there was an accelerated change to open treeless vegetation, grasses and ribwort plantain, courtesy of deteriorating weather conditions, forcing inhabitants to adapt the land to agriculture and the use of wood for heat.

A substantial community was thriving at the time at Ness of Brodgar, a 2.5 hectare complex of large structures built of fine drystone masonry and roofed with thin stone slabs, all contained within a six-foot protective wall. A series of elegant stone dwellings with a central temple suggests a group of people living aside and behaving very differently from the general population. Its position on the narrow isthmus between Stenness, a second stone circle, and a straight-line ceremonial route linking with another settlement at Skara Brae is highly suggestive of a holy order, of a people involved in the pursuit of something sacred, perhaps a priesthood of sorts.[6]

A further rise in sea level around 3000 BC sculpted the shoreline and formed a series of lochs throughout Orkney, with relatively shallow channels between the islands, making the short ferry rides today either hair-raising or spirited, depending on your appetite for risk. It took a series of catastrophic changes to the climate to finally force the dwellers of Orkney to seek a more predictable environment on mainland Scotland, as seen by the decommissioning in 2450 BC of the Ness of Brodgar. Following an elaborate ceremony involving a massive feast, the removal of internal features and the dismantling of drystone walls, the entire site was carefully and ritually buried. Then, its nameless conclave moved on and vanished into thin air.

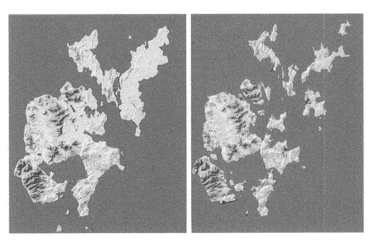

Going, going.... Sea level rises from 8000-5000 BC.

Might they have been responsible for erecting the nearby stones? It is unusual for anyone familiar with temple protocol to place a habitation in-between sacred sites, so there is a possibility the complex was a later addition, least of all because the size of the lintels used in the construction of Structure 27 suggest they might have been re-purposed from Stenness itself.

Regardless, whoever lived on Orkney certainly possessed an uncanny ability to build impressive stone circles. Walking the ceremonial route from Stenness and past the Ness of Brodgar, one sees along the ridge a long line of dark fingers reaching to the sky: the second stone circle, the Ring of Brodgar.

On approach, one first pays respect to a lone, outlying megalith – the Comet Stone. Nicknamed 'the fiddler', it is the subject of an ancient folk tale. The circle was said to originally have been a nocturnal meeting place for giants, but they had to return home before dawn lest they turn to stone. One night a fiddler struck up a tune so lusty it had the giants dancing. The faster he fiddled, the faster the giants cut the rug. In their excitement they forgot to keep

18th century panorama of Brodgar.

an eye on the rising Sun, and as morning broke they were all turned to stone. But worse was to come. When the music stopped so did the rhythm of the land. The moral of the story is that failure to pay attention to the function of the sacred site and its connection with the rhythm of life leads to an imbalance in the natural order, causing the land to fall into ruin.

A number of massive standing stones around Orkney are coupled with traditions of giants. On the island of North Ronaldsay there used to be a stone with a hole high on its face that was said to have been found on the shore by a giant woman, who pushed her finger through the hole and carried the stone to the top of the hill. Another stone on Rousay was given the Norse name Yernasteen (Giant's Stone), and was regularly used by local people as a site of veneration.

At first, the stones of the Ring of Brodgar appear equally spaced, yet when the circle is approached from either causeway it is obvious that they have been manipulated. Either side of the two entrances, the monoliths are broader and closer together, so that the scale of the circle, already massive to begin with, is further enhanced. Overall the circle still has twenty-seven of its original sandstones upright, making it a wonder to experience in its near perfection. Estimates for the total number of original stones range from forty to sixty, with fifty-six the most likely, as this is the specific number of stones originally employed at sites such as Stonehenge, which serve to synchronize solar and lunar cycles and calculate eclipses.[7] Properly reconstructed, Brodgar would still be an accurate calendar thousands of years into the future.

The choice of setting offers a panoramic view of the two lochs either side of the ridge, while in the distance the looming Ward Hill on Hoy watches like a patient master. It's as close as anyone will come these days to experiencing the serenity generated by a harmonious interaction between a Neolithic sacred space and its engirding landscape. Some of Brodgar's sandstones were naturally extracted, others deliberately shaped into trapezoids and triangles as though strategically tracking the movement of objects in the sky, giving the site a feeling totally different to Stenness. This is a practical place, a site for measuring things.

It is surprising that this perfect 331-foot diameter circle is the largest in Scotland – the third largest in Britain – yet so little is known about it and so few excavations have ever been conducted. The British Army took a more active interest when they used it to practice tank maneuvers during World War II. One of the few academics to actively engage with the site was the engineer Alexander Thom who, while surveying it in 1976, posed the following question: "Why was a more level site not chosen?" Indeed Brodgar is not on the summit of the ridge, nor is it placed on a more architecturally suitable location. It's as though the builders, while making obvious

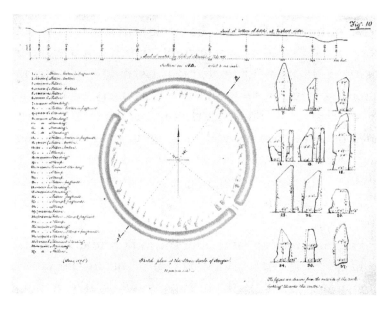

use of the unobstructed view of the sky, also put it there to form part of an interconnected whole. This seemingly innocuous remark compelled me to see Brodgar not as a lone monument but as working in conjunction with Stenness, and perhaps other nearby monuments as well.

During his time here, Thom experienced his own "Eureka!" moment when he discovered that the engineers of Brodgar had constructed the monument using a specific unit of measure — dubbed the Megalithic Yard — which Thom applied with remarkable accuracy to hundreds of other stone circles from Scotland to Brittany, proving that a large swathe of monuments was built according to the same recipe.[8]

Stranger still is how the megalith builders arrived at the numerical value behind this unit of measure. 1 Megalithic Yard equals 2.72 feet. The same value is found in the ratio of the surface area of a tetrahedron relative to its circumscribing sphere, the two geometric forms behind every atomic structure, the very glue of the molecular universe, whose discovery was only made possible with the invention of the electron microscope. Which begs the question, did Neolithic architects stumble upon this by chance? Or was it a coincidence, like when they chose the exact center of the Ring of Brodgar to mark 59° 00' latitude?

While Stenness impresses with its linear, machine-like presence, Brodgar demonstrates the expertise of an astute engineer. Its surrounding 403-foot diameter ditch is 30 feet wide by 12 feet deep. 166,000 cubic feet of material was expertly chiseled out of solid bedrock using an estimated 80,000 hours of labor to create a distinct and deep moat which is always full of water.[9] Causeways on the southeast and northwest sections are the only way in. The site also appears to have been deliberately placed to take advantage of a natural spring at the center, which not only feeds the semi-pervious rock but, in times when the bedrock was exposed, created a mirror with which to measure the sky. Ancient Vedic astronomers used precisely the same technique, as did their Egyptian counterparts, who created geodetically-placed sacred mounds surrounded by water from where they made accurate calculations of stars, assisted by the gold plated points of pillars and obelisks, from which calculations were transposed onto the landscape and transfixed by temples.[10]

It seems odd that recent efforts to date the Ring of Brodgar involved digging two trenches into the ditch, yet no one thought to take samples from beneath the stones, which would provide a better idea of when they might have been erected. Having fallen into disuse for the better part of four thousand years, the ditch filled up with silt, soil, broken stones, pollen and decaying plant matter. When archaeologists reached the bottom they found dusty silt and rubified minerals, evidence of the ditch having been periodically cleaned — the proper housekeeping one would expect after all the effort employed in building Brodgar – while subsequent layers showed a gradual build-up of plant matter, rubble and peat, suggesting the site

eventually fell into disuse. The date range provided from carbon-dating was wide, from 3700 BC to as late as 1600 BC.[11] If we assume the oldest date signifies a period of initial decay and disuse, it follows that Brodgar is considerably older, certainly more than six thousand years.[12]

To get a sense of the true age of Brodgar and Stenness one needs to continue walking further up the ridge, to a third site that everyone ignores. If there's one thing I've learned from interacting with Mysteries teachings it's that you always pay attention to seemingly innocuous details – things low on the eye candy spectrum – as it is there that you find the key to unlocking all kinds of secrets. As it turns out I was already two-thirds to a solution.

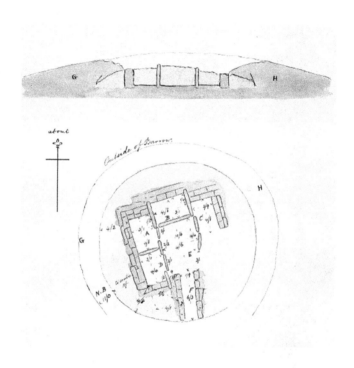

Petrie's sketch of the chambered mound in the center of the Ring of Bookan, 1861.

3

TWO THIRDS
OF A RIDDLE

he traveling antiquarian Frederick Thomas visited Orkney around 1848 and was overawed by what he saw. He also offered candid advice to future generations to protect the rich collection of antiquities from the ignoble fate that had already befallen so many, advice that in hindsight would have saved hundreds of monuments. Writing in his journal, Thomas exclaims: "The following Notes have been arranged partly with the view of affording the means for comparing the Celtic antiquities of the Orkneys with their prototypes situated in other countries, but more particularly in the hope of inducing some resident gentleman of more leisure and antiquarian lore to draw up a detailed description of these interesting Landmarks of Time, many of which are fast disappearing before the efforts of rural industry and agricultural improvement. There is, however, but little cause to apprehend any further dilapidation in the greater monuments of the county; an interest in their conservation is daily gaining strength, and we have the faith to believe that in a short time even a peasant will feel ashamed to remove from the

inquiring presence of enlightened men an irrecoverable record of the thoughts and feelings of a by-gone race. The antiquities of the Orkney and Shetland groups will be found upon examination to be well worthy of a careful study, not only from being extremely numerous for the small extent of country in which they are placed, but also from the great diversity of their forms, in many places leaving us unable to determine the purpose for which they have been erected."[1]

If visibility and altitude are determining factors in selecting the optimum location for an observatory, then given the scale of the Ring of Brodgar it seems odd that this stone circle was not constructed on the highest elevation along the isthmus separating the two lochs. Instead that position is occupied by a third site, an inconspicuous mound and ditch by the name Ring of Bookan, of which Thomas further remarked: "the Ring of Bûkan is a circular space surrounded by a deep excavated trench, thus far resembling the Ring of Brogar, but it wants the circumferential stones, and besides the interior shews evident marks of superstructure. Many stones of small size are apparently in situ, yet no order could be traced among them; one is erect, about three feet in height, and one-foot square. A triangular-shaped block, making a comfortable seat, occupies the centre, while another, completely identical in size and figure, is prostrate upon the circumference of the ring. Within the area there is the appearance of five or six small tangential circles about six feet in diameter, and formed of earth; within these the stumps of stones are prominent; the whole is too obscure to admit of any statement concerning it to be made with certainty, but I conjecture that these compartments are the remains of small cromlechs long since destroyed."[2]

As I walked the site during a rare moment of uninterrupted sunshine, I came to appreciate the value of

Thomas' observations. The deep moat is no longer deep, it has silted to the point where it is barely discernible. The stones "lying prostrate along the perimeter of the ring" are all gone save for two outliers, with a third reemployed as a fence post. Another sacred space, another quarry, much like the fate of Stenness two miles downhill.

Bookan is officially regarded as a mound and ditch rather than a stone circle, yet Thomas' account clearly implies it may originally have been one. The same argument was used by archaeologists at a similar site at Knowlton in England, until a group of schoolchildren on an outing to learn the ancient art of dowsing located parts of the still-buried stone circle, proving that one should never underestimate the deductive power of teenagers armed with bent coat hangers.[3]

Whether the central mound and chamber was originally part of the circle remains unclear. Sites such as these have a rich history of being recycled for burial to confer high status by association upon the deceased. 'I am buried in a sacred site therefore I, too, am a god'. The chamber was excavated around 1861 by antiquarian James Farrer, whose inexperienced workmen caused much damage, but in their defense the chamber was found to have been previously disturbed, "with the upper part in an especially ruinous state," as noted by George Petrie, the archaeologist who accompanied Farrer. Formed by flagstones set on edge, the surviving mound has a height of six feet and a diameter of forty four. The chamber's load-bearing orthostats are 2.8 feet tall, with a central

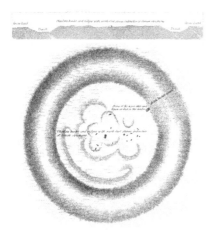

Thomas' survey of Bookan, 1849.

chamber a foot lower and about as wide. The passage was clearly not intended as a crawl space, nor was it a burial site, as it would have allowed vermin access to a body for whom so much effort had been spent in preserving for posterity. Its south south-westerly orientation is not an alignment traditionally associated with burial; according to the rules of sacred space, the deceased are typically laid west to east or placed north-south so that the soul may be reborn in the region of rejuvenation, the Pole Star.[4] Even Petrie himself was skeptical, noting that the cairn was stuffed with mixed skeletal remains and designed so out of character with traditional chambered cairns as to allow for the suspicion that it was appropriated long after its original function had ceased.[5]

If anything, given its elevation and selective view of the horizon, the stone passage is more indicative of a light box marking a stellar event whose light or relationship to the site symbolically impregnates the mound. A proper excavation was finally undertaken in 2005, but with so much of the site having been previously contaminated, the only usable radiocarbon date was a bone fragment from 1900-1800 BC. The general archaeological consensus is that Bookan was likely built c.4500 BC, fell into disuse by 2900-2500 BC, and thereafter monumentalized for

Two surviving stones frame the gap in the hills on Hoy.

the deposition of human remains.[6] It is also possible that the stones used for the original circle were broken up and reused to expand the light box into a series of ceremonial niches, because Petrie's sketches of the angular stones inside the chamber are surmounted by a three-foot raised cairn that is contained by three concentric revetment walls into which several human ribs were mixed.

Bookan's vantage point allows a view along the isthmus towards Brodgar and Stenness, whenever the weather is calm enough to allow it. Since this was one such rare occasion I took the opportunity between gales and horizontal rain to walk the site, eat lunch and let the spirit of place tell me its story.

It certainly had something to convey. Standing at the entrance to the now-collapsed chamber, the eye is magnetically drawn to the pregnant belly that is Hoy, with the steep cleft between Ward Hill and Knap of Twoieglen giving the mountains the resemblance of Earth Mother's fertile breasts. The natural symbolism couldn't be more obvious, yet the passage chamber is not distracted by this. Instead it looks to the left, towards a thin crescent of horizon formed by the interweaving of the lowlands of Orkney and the tip of Hoy. There's no doubt this was a deliberate intention on the part of the ancient surveyor because this natural bowl is suggestive of a hollow from which an object is supposed to rise. The Sun or Moon, perhaps a constellation. I make a note to book another scintillating ferry ride to Hoy, with some life insurance on the side.

Indeed, something important is going on here. The alignment of Bookan, Brodgar and Stenness follows a general south-easterly trajectory of 129°. Plotting the coordinates gives a potential correspondence to the winter solstice sunrise c.6800 BC. This was surprising because no one should have been building such structures this early and so far north, even though one local archaeological site has provided a radiocarbon date for human activity around 6600 BC.[7] Looking closer, the three sites are not in perfect alignment – Stenness is askew from the others, or seen in reverse, Bookan is off-kilter. Any alignment is therefore redundant, and the answer lies elsewhere. It was at this moment that a vivid snapshot of the belt stars of Orion presented itself in my mind. Could this be what the architects had intended? I drove back to Stenness, took bearings, returned to Bookan. Double-checked the map. No doubt about it, the three sites appear to be mimicking the three stars and the distinctive kink of their alignment.

The weather predictably closed in once again, the fields of green taking on the pallor of ash. Nothing more to do for the day except retire to the bed and breakfast, where my generous hosts poured me liberal portions of 'research', otherwise known in the trade as fine whisky. A couple of *drams* later (one should only use the elixir to

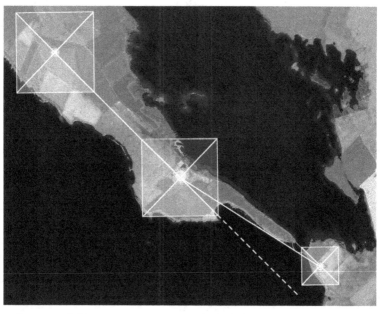

Survey of Giza pyramids overlaid on the three stone circles.

lubricate the machinery, not over-oil it), I was keen to grab my computer and find out what the sky above Stenness, Brodgar and Bookan looked like thousands of years ago and whether it could establish a probable date of construction.

With the sky racing backwards in time, courtesy of an addictive astronomy program called Stellarium, I waited for a possible Orkney-Orion correlation to appear. The same theory has already been proposed at Giza by Robert Bauval and Adrian Gilbert.[8] On a hunch I overlaid an accurate survey of the three pyramids over the Orkney stone circles and was surprised to see the same spatial relationship is consistent between the two, right down to the tip of each pyramid referencing the center of each circle. This was very encouraging. Now all that was required was a marker in the sky above Orkney.

The typical markers for sky-ground temple relationships fall disproportionally on two specific times of the year: the winter solstice and the spring equinox. Tracking the sky back 8000 years revealed that the Sun and the chamber of Bookan were not designed to meet. The Moon, on the other hand, is referenced at its Major Standstill when it makes a brief appearance a few degrees above the horizon – but barely so. But what of Orion?

As the program slowly rotated the heavens in the era of 6600 BC – the earliest known sign of human activity in this region – Orion still lay below the horizon, so nothing doing there.

Time for another wee *dram*. When Petrie attended the excavation of Bookan he made a sketch of its stone passage and in doing so handed us a great gift. From the drawing one is able to calculate the average line of sight at 175° south south-west, give or take a couple of degrees. As the planets and stars kept revolving on my screen, nothing significant was taking place. Then on the evening of the winter solstice in 5300 BC, the three belt stars rise for the first time above the only available window on the horizon, cutting a narrow arc over the island of Hoy for a brief thirty minutes before sliding behind the hills. So this is what the light box at Bookan was looking at so long ago.

But Orkney's ancient architects had something more on their mind. The smaller of the three belt stars, Mintaka, is seen on the right. On the ground, the circle of Stenness is the smaller of the three and is therefore assumed to be the terrestrial counterpart of Mintaka. Taking a bird's eye-view looking south, Orion's Belt is seen mirrored in reverse by the three stone circles – a sky-ground relationship of which any ancient Egyptian would be proud.

Incidentally, a southward trajectory of 126° through Brodgar and Stenness leads you directly to Giza.

If a group of astronomers living on Orkney over seven thousand years ago built such an extraordinary sky-ground alignment of monuments, what else might they have created with the other sites scattered throughout this archipelago?

Station Stone by Loch Stenness, its angled ledge a common feature of many megaliths. Hoy beckons in the distance.

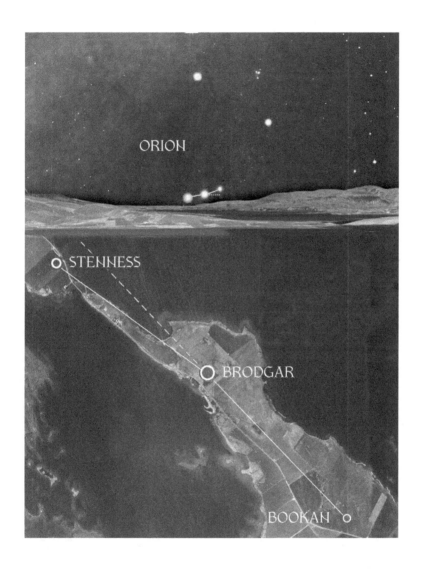

*One of the stones of Stenness angled towards
the natural bowl into which the Sun, Moon
and Orion's Belt descend.*

4

AN ORCADIAN SAGA

he Orkney archipelago has been called
the Egypt of the North on account of the
disproportionate number of Neolithic
sacred sites – 3000 at last count – relative
to its territory. The closest comparative example is the
archipelago of Malta.

Orkney's coastline is gradually yet surely submerging.
There is no doubt that beneath shallow waters lie the
remains of earlier sites, and with them a larger
civilization footprint. One circular structure has been
identified under Loch Harray, beside the Ring of Brodgar
– a potential precursor to the stone circle, as though the
builders were seeking higher ground. Barely three miles
to the east, a submerged 120-foot mound and a series of
megalithic structures exist in what is now the Bay of
Firth. Archaeologist Caroline Wikham-Jones believes
that, given the amount of drowned coastline, the number
of submerged sites may be substantial.[1]

One passage mound by the name Point of Cott has
lost half its bulk since 1935 as the Atlantic slowly but
inexorably nibbles it away into the sea, and yet the same

storms that perpetually bash the islands are paradoxically revealing Neolithic habitations, left in an excellent state of preservation thanks to thousands of years of protective cover by sand dunes and grass.

One of the joys of exploring the archipelago is the rare privilege of experiencing a rich Neolithic heritage in peace and quiet, save for the automatic chomping of grass by sheep which, I have to admit, sounds relaxing *in situ*. When the rain inevitably comes, there is always the option of retiring for a *dram*, watching the weather turn, and returning once more to your chores.

Incidentally, the much-celebrated *dram* is not a Scottish word at all but an Armenian import, and in both places it means the same thing.

Back in the fields, I wandered off from Stenness – now barely seven feet above sea level – to make friends with a lone standing stone on the next ridge before continuing to the imposing and elegant chambered mound of Maeshowe and its encircling ditch. From above it looks like an exercise ball was dropped by a butter-fingered god and left a single ripple that in its time was filled with water. According to the *Orkneyinga* saga, in 1153 a group of Viking warriors once sought shelter from a blizzard inside the spacious chamber: "Earl Harald set out for Orkney at Christmas with four ships and a hundred men. He lay for two days off Graemsay then put in at Hamnavoe on Hrossey [Mainland Orkney], and on the thirteenth day of Christmas they travelled on foot over to Firth. During a snowstorm they took shelter in Orkahaugr [Maeshowe] and there two of them went insane, which slowed them down badly, so that by the time they reached Firth it was night-time." Before leaving, one obliging Viking carved the following runic inscription on the chamber wall: JÓRSALAFARAR BRUTU ORKHAUG (JERUSALEM-TRAVELLERS [CRUSADERS] BROKE ORK MOUND).[2] Early Christians have claimed Maeshowe was burgled and looted by bloodthirsty Norwegians, but now, thanks to graffiti, we have the other side of the story. Accounts of Vikings as nothing more than marauding barbarians began circulating around the time Christianity migrated to the isles of Scotland, yet new research suggests that much of the contact was based on friendly trade and settlement. The history of human conquest is awash with incomers portraying others as evildoers, and in this case the misconception centers around Scandinavian settlers being lumped into the same stew as *vikingr*, 'pirates', and left to suffer the consequences of this malicious exercise in public relations.

By the time Christian looters broke into Maeshowe the entrance was no longer visible, forcing them to seek entry by digging a hole through the roof. Consequently the mound we see today is 13 feet shorter than its original height. Prior to its official excavation in 1861 – ironically using the same hole to gain entry – Maeshowe's exterior also looked very different to the soft, spherical shape we see today. In a letter to *The Orcadian* newspaper, George Petrie describes the mound as 36-foot high with a "bluntly conical outline" and a deep depression in the top.[3]

Maeshowe, with lochs Harray and Stenness, 1862.

Watercolors painted around this time show Maeshowe to be just so, its profile bearing a resemblance to the Phrygian cap worn by worshippers of the ancient cult of Mithras, centered in and around Asia Minor. Indeed, there may be more than a passing observation here because, architecturally, the inside of Maeshowe shares more in common with passage mounds of Mycenia and the *kurgans* of the Black Sea region than it does with Scotland.[4] *Kurgan* derives from the Armenian word *kura-garq*, 'crucible of the social class', which in the context of a circular building denotes a meeting place for high ranking people – a select priesthood, if you like – and tallies well with etymology found in later Sumerian language. A second possibility, *kura-grag*, 'crucible of fire energy', implies an astronomical connection and ties in nicely with Maeshowe's alignment, as we shall see.

For decades it was generally accepted that Maeshowe and its circular bank were contemporary works, but radiocarbon dating proves otherwise. For one thing, the mound was erected upon an existing artificial platform. While the bank and platform suggest a date of 3990 BC, the mound itself dates to 2820 BC, a discrepancy of over one thousand years.[5] Since the latter results are based entirely on bone fragments found inside the mound rather than the organic material of the mound itself we are left no wiser as to its true age, only that it was likely decommissioned at that time, sealed, and human remains deposited within. The date is also consistent with the decommissioning of nearby Ness of Brodgar and its deliberate burial, providing a snapshot of a culture that appears to have completed a phase of its allotted work and moved elsewhere. This was common practice throughout ancient temple culture whenever the cycle and purpose of a building had run its course. Case in point: Cairnpapple, originally a henge on the Scottish mainland, was re-

1862 excavation. The corner uprights resemble those of Stenness, and serve no structural purpose.

purposed as a burial site a thousand years after its initial construction.

But let's return to the artificial platform upon which Maeshowe stands. At the edge of it, two large sockets once contained a pair of standing stones even larger than those at nearby Stenness, which appear to have been aligned to the rising midwinter Sun. Did the mound builders engage in a kind of stone cannibalism? Since no further excavation has been carried out it is impossible to prove the that two stones formed part of a previous circle whose stones were recycled to build Maeshowe's interior passage.[6] However, to cite one of many examples of this practice, in Carnac, whose structures are believed to have been precursors to Scotland's, the notable passage mounds of Gavrinis, Table des Marchand and Kercado utilize menhirs extracted from the megalithic site of Er Grah.[7]

Proper access into Maeshowe is made via a low and narrow thirty-foot-long passageway. The front section consists of vertical layers of small irregular stones fitted like a field wall, whereas the rear, by contrast, is formed of industrially-fitted megalithic slabs, indicating that the front was extended at a later period by a stone mason with different abilities. The rear section is strangely reminiscent of the passage leading into the Queen's Chamber of the Great Pyramid of Giza, right down to the width and height.

As a whole, the passage is divided by a door jamb, beyond which is a triangular alcove with a large triangular stone, slightly narrower than the width of the passage, allowing it to fit perfectly into the recess, provoking the archaeologist George Petrie to write the following observation: "This block suggests the idea that it had been used to shut up the passage... and that it was pushed back into the recess in the wall when admission into the chamber was desired."[8]

Anyone who has seen the blocking stone will agree that moving it in and out is not a simple task; it would be much easier to maneuver if sealing the passage from the inside, implying the chamber was used for some unspecified ritual, or perhaps the conduct of exclusive affairs. During his excavation James Farrer makes no

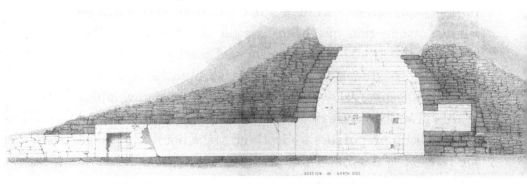

Maeshowe passage and inner chamber, with hole in the ceiling where the less scrupulous forced an entry.

mention of human remains except for a small fragment of human skull, while Petrie himself refers to several skull fragments. Suffice it to say there was not a huge quantity of bone to justify Maeshowe being classified as a burial site. By comparison, the Quanterness chambered cairn of 3400 BC, a few miles to the east, was found packed with human remains.[9]

Having done my best to imitate a crouching chimpanzee, I joined the site's caretaker in the central chamber – a water-tight, high-roofed corbelled room with three small side-chambers set into the masonry three feet above the floor. The excavators of 1861 found this beautiful room to be "completely filled with the stones which had originally formed the upper part of the walls and roof, and with the clay which had completed the top of the tumulus."[10]

Like me, Farrer's excavators found the quality of the dry-stone masonry impeccable, the walls rising 4.6 feet before a magnificent corbelled roof slopes inwards to form a kind of beehive. The height of the original roof is estimated at 19.6 feet – a measurement that is oddly consistent in monuments throughout the Scottish Isles. Four monoliths stand like stoic sentinels at each corner, fifteen feet tall, angled and pointed like the stones of Stenness. They serve no structural purpose, and since the chamber was built up around them, the stones were a planned feature from the outset. They were erected first and stood in the open landscape as Maeshowe rose.[10] Perhaps there was an earlier structure here after all, a stone circle much like Stenness, as suggested; or perhaps the architect was inspired by the style of its angled megaliths. Or inspired by a visit to the Mediterranean even, because he or she reproduced, in miniature and in temperament, a chamber from the Red Pyramid at Dahshur, or for that matter, similar chambers found throughout Sardinia.

Alignment plays a key role in deciphering when a temple might have been built as well as in understanding its purpose. In the case of Maeshowe the main passage faces southwest and, as every tour guide points out, towards the setting midwinter Sun. Except the two don't quite line up nowadays. Due to the effects of a natural phenomenon called *precession*, with each passing millennia the Sun and stars rise and set in different places along the horizon, so much so that a modern-day visitor inside Maeshowe will not witness the beam of the Sun reaching the rear niche on the winter solstice unless they stay on for three more weeks.

Six thousand years ago it was a very different story. Maeshowe's passageway and its 5° angle of view is designed to frame the cleft made by the imposing slopes of Ward Hill and Knap of Trowieglen on the distant island of Hoy. Together with the foreground of southern Orkney, they combine to form a natural and unmistakable bowl. Taking the earliest radiocarbon date of 3990 BC at face value, the midwinter Sun would have set into this bowl and shone true down the passage of Maeshowe, assuming the mound was already built by this date and the alignment was marked by the original standing stones.

Trajectories of Sun, Moon and Orion's Belt into the bowl, 3990 BC.

A second object follows the Sun's trajectory into the bowl: the setting Moon at its Minor Standstill, consecrating the cosmic marriage of the solar masculine and lunar feminine. But there's more. On the night of the winter solstice, Orion's Belt is seen descending into the bowl, a performance repeated once again on the spring equinox.

The surprise here is that ancient people rarely, if ever commemorated or celebrated the setting of objects in the sky, but rather the rising or mid-heaven positions, when the energy and power of such 'gods' were deemed to be at their most abundant. Much in the same way no one celebrates an empty glass of Scotch. This glitch at Maeshowe has been bugging me for years, leading me to speculate that the mound's reference of the setting Sun and other celestial objects must have been important to people for whom this was culturally significant, and as far as I'm aware, the Egyptians and Armenians are the two rare cultures known to honor the setting Sun.

Could this have been the true purpose behind Maeshowe? In the ritual calendar, the south-western orientation of a temple celebrates harvest — the giving of thanks to the spirit of the land for providing an abundant supply of food, which, on an island known for its short

The interior passage.

growing season, would be cause enough for celebration. Or perhaps there's another, yet undiscovered, reason.

It was late in the day. My allotted time with the caretaker had run its course, and as she prepared to close the chamber I took the opportunity to kneel and look out along the shaft of the passageway. The pallid light of rainfall had surrendered to gleaming sunlight. The midwinter Sun might no longer align, but, unlike the stars, the immovable hulk of Hoy will always stare back. An angled stone at Stenness points to its natural chalice. It is referenced by a ledge cut into the nearby Station Stone. Even the tallest megaliths on Brodgar's southwest quadrant frame it.

It was time to take the ferry.

Braving the short ride across the shallow and truculent waters to Hoy is a kind of life accomplishment, an initiation, something to brag about to Odin on your way to Valhalla. Before a dramatic rise in sea level around 3000 BC, this channel would have been a series of shallow inlets, most of them easily forded. Nowadays the open ferry accommodates only a handful of vehicles. As I stood on deck, bracing against the gale while attempting to film the dramatic scenery, I wondered why people remained inside their vehicles instead of standing outside admiring what is, undoubtedly, a formidable example of prehistoric scenery, complete with Ridley Scott-style shafts of light among squalls of dark grey and orange cloud. When my feet became submerged in seawater I understood why the boat is designed with large holes around an open deck: to offer passage to waves so they wash through the boat.

Always learn from the locals.

Once on dry land and the only road along the length of Hoy, the valley separating the Knap of Trowieglen and Ward Hill is brooding territory, covered in bracken and bog. And legends. It is said that near the summit of Ward Hill something very bright is seen shining and sparkling from May to July, observed even from Orkney, but although many have climbed the hill in search of it no explanation has been forthcoming.

Perseverance and a stout pair of Wellingtons delivers you through the bog and halfway up the hill to two titanic, isolated blocks of Devonian red sandstone. The one further along appears to have had part of its face shaped by hand into a semi-circular bowl, although it is hard to tell because much of it is still covered with mud and heather.

The other is called the Dwarfie Stane. With laser-like precision some unidentified stonemason sliced a hole about three-feet square, then continued for eight feet into the solid slab. To the left, a semi-circular chamber some five feet long features a raised lip on the floor as though meant to hold a thin layer of liquid. To the right is a

Dwarfie Stane.

51

similar chamber bordered by what can only be described as a rectangular picture frame meant to prevent someone or something from falling out. Carved along the base of the rear wall is what appears to be a stone bolster.

The feeling inside this hollow world is not so much of claustrophobia as of omnipresence. You can hear your breath as much as your heart – you become instantly aware of your mortality. I have been inside many chambers in the world and crawled along narrow passages under pyramids, but I can say this experience, above all others, is disarming. What on earth were people doing in here?

Part of the answer rests outside the entrance, where lies a large sandstone plug used to seal the entrance, leaving but a sliver of a gap to allow oxygen to pass inside. If someone were meant to have been buried inside here, they hardly would have needed air to breathe. Quite how this plug was cut from the main slab and then from the back is a mystery – or perhaps the plug was fashioned from identical stone with identical veins and made to fit precisely. Either way a lot of effort was employed to create a womb from a slab of sandstone in a remote and

Dwarfie Stane, central chamber.

otherwise featureless valley. When unnamed visitors came here prior to the 16th century – maybe the same "crusaders" fingered by the Vikings – they found the Dwarfie Stane still plugged. Unable to dislodge it, they broke in by smashing a hole in the roof, for which they were compensated with a treasure of ... nothing. So much, then, for the tomb theory.

Local legends accredit the work to a dwarf, while another contradictorily attributes it to a giant. But perhaps the most revealing information about the Dwarfie Stane comes from a 19th century graffito carved in both English and Persian on the south exterior face by one William Mounsey. Captain Mounsey had been posted to the Middle East where he took a passionate interest in Persian and Egyptian cultures. By the time he returned to England he'd become a mystic, and his veneration of sacred places defined his later life as an antiquarian. Which leads us to his carving: "I HAVE SAT TWO NIGHTS AND SO LEARNT PATIENCE."

Did Mounsey miss a bus? Was he stranded on Hoy for two nights and resorted to using the chamber for shelter?

Dwarfie Stane, right chamber.

To someone who's researched and practiced the mystical arts for a considerable period, it is very clear what Mounsey was conveying to visitors: the chamber is used for shamanic travel, the ultimate test of patience. The clue here is the entrance's precise alignment due West, the ritual direction to the spirit world – Annwn to the Gaelic people. With several hours at my disposal before catching the return ferry, I decided to go meet this Celtic Otherworld.

Lying flat in each of the cavities, I noted how they were designed to generate a perfect resonance, and a very, very low one at that. There are two other places I know where such a low note, performed appropriately, reaches the same desired effect: one is West Kennett Long Barrow in England, a passage mound where people practiced exactly the same ritual and, coincidentally where the bones of very, very tall people were interred. The other is the box in the King's Chamber of the Great Pyramid.

Sustaining the low note for only a couple of minutes, I was already halfway out-of-body. It rapidly became difficult to maintain a grasp on consciousness. Given that a ferry was waiting, I practiced and recorded the sound for ten minutes before concluding that if I stayed, I, like Mounsey, would discover patience inside the Dwarfie Stane whilst traveling into the Otherworld for two nights.

So this is the object to which all those sites on Orkney are pointing. If this assumption is correct then what we are dealing with here on the northern limits of the world is the beginning of an intentionally designed ritual landscape.

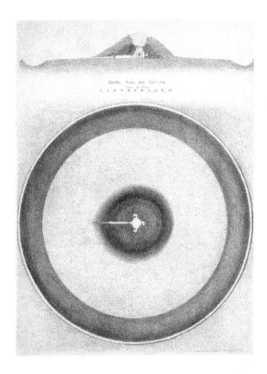

Maeshowe.

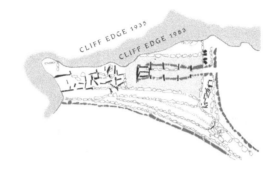

Point of Cott, a horned mound eroded by rising seas.

A DESIGNED
LANDSCAPE

ndeed, the number of passage mounds in Orkney, along with the Outer Hebridean islands of Lewis, Harris, Benbecula, and North and South Uist, is staggering given the remoteness and low population density of the territory. It is as though a group of people migrated from elsewhere under duress, wishing to recreate a world familiar to them while remaining isolated from mainland Britain.

Early attempts at understanding the nature of the mounds and other structures met with considerable difficulty because of the lack of parallels in the region. The possibility that a megalithic culture might have been imported was rarely entertained, even though a short journey across the English Channel to Brittany reveals thousands of mounds exhibiting the same qualities, many of them created in earlier epochs and facing the same issue of rising seas that forced its culture further inland.

Antiquarians and academics argued that the Scottish structures were built for defensive purposes, even as dwellings for migrating Picts, and when historians such as George Barry expressed the opinion that these "had not been destined for the abode of men,"[1] every mound was assumed to have accommodated the dead. This is myopic thinking at its best, based on guesswork and conjecture. Purloining other peoples' masterwork is an ancient pastime. Persian kings and Egyptian pharaohs were particularly prone to recycling places of antiquity because the association conferred immediate god-like status at a fraction of the cost to erect similar buildings themselves. With changing customs and circumstances, a passage mound once used for restricted ceremony or astronomical calculation could be appropriated for storage, a place of hiding, a place of habitation, and, yes, a place of rest for a dignitary. It took until the late 20th century for archaeologists with new vision, such as Colin Renfrew and Anna Ritchie, to further the understanding of the western isles' Neolithic culture, yet still the ghost of a burial cult that made sacrifices to a supreme being hovers over their educated conclusions.

Going walkabout on the Orkney archipelago spoils you with lone interaction with many mounds and standing stones, making it easier to experience moments of introspection, to hear the spirit of place transfer its memory. Such transactions are deeply personal: you really do feel intimately engaged with the land and its history, something above and beyond any intellectual pursuit. The eroded condition of the sites makes them less photogenic, so visitors and selfie seekers are

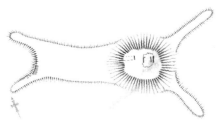

Head of Work horned mound.

Point of Cott horned mound.

sparse. Near Vestra Fiold (one of the quarry sites for the stone circles) lies one such heavily weathered chambered cairn whose design is really out of place in this part of the world – a pre-excavation survey of the mound found its northern end to consist of two projecting horns. Nor is this the only example of such a design on Orkney. Due east from the Ring of Bookan lies a second chambered mound on the oddly named Head of Work, or to use the full name, Headland of the village of Work. A bulbous cairn was extended at the front and rear to form a 130 foot-long horned mound; or if you prefer, a crescent was added at both ends. Thanks to the existence of an accurate survey, it is easy to calculate that its chamber marks the equinox sunrise c.5000 BC.

A third horned mound, Point of Cott, was identified on the northern island of Westray. Despite its eastern side now being partly obliterated by the encroaching sea, enough of its bulk remains to offer a good idea of what it once looked like: an elongated horned mound built around a 24-foot-long rectangular orthostatic box[2] – a feature less at home in Britain and more so in Carnac or Sardinia. The radiocarbon dates secured from a human skull and birds found here yielded a wild range of 3650-1650 BC,[3] but the south-facing chamber contradicts this by pointing to the first rising of Orion's Belt on the winter solstice c.5300 BC.

So far, these mounds appear to be contemporaries of the stone circles. As I marked them on a map it became clear that the first two horned mounds are equidistant from Point of Cott and collectively form a perfect isosceles triangle, a flat pyramid designed across the landscape.

I couldn't help bisecting the angles to see what might lie at the center. The exact crossing occurs on the island of Ramsay, at the base of a steep hill marked by Knowe of Lairo, a 130-foot-long horned passage mound with a tripartite chamber.

It is quite an effort to position four remote objects accurately using GPS alone, but to do so without technology across 340 square miles of undulating terrain, over waterways, and with hills blocking your line of sight, is impressive.

Curious as to what else the triangle's bisecting lines might be referencing, I followed the north-south line from Point of Cott through Knowe of Lairo to where it meets the lower arm of the triangle. The spot is marked by the summit of Ward of Redland, the highest point of a range of hills. From this pointed ridge one has an unobstructed view over northern Orkney, and on a clear day it is possible to see three of the four mounds. The location is a surveyor's dream, and deemed sufficiently important for the construction lines and their trajectories to remain marked to this day by field boundaries.

No less than five surviving mounds and *brochs* (ancient hollow-walled towers) mark the full trajectory of the lower arm of the triangle.

Heading north from Head of Work to Point of Cott, the east arm passes through a mound on the tiny outcrop of what is now

Field boundaries mark the triangle's lines of contact.

the island of Helliar Holm. It then crosses the sea and makes landfall at a chambered mound at the tip of the island of Egilsay, returning to the sea before reaching the shore of Westray, where it is welcomed by a half-eroded passage mound, with part of its fine internal wall still visible above the sand.

From Point of Cott southwards, the western arm passes beside Howa Tower, a chambered cairn on a rise near the coast, then continues along the sea to Orkney and the summit of a hill – another perfect surveying

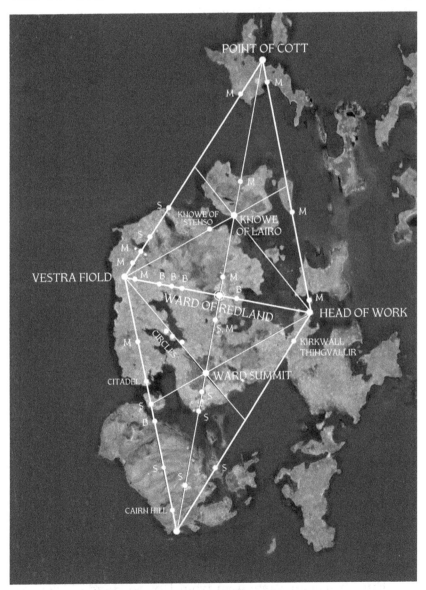

The Orkney Triangle and its mirror image.
M= mound; S= summit; B= broch.

position – continues on to another summit, passes through two adjacent mounds, both aligned to the line's trajectory, before arriving at the crest of the hill and the mounds of Vestra Fiold.

Incidentally, the bisecting line from Vestra Fiold to the center of the triangle passes right through the ruins of a habitation called Knowe of Stenso, a once impressive *broch* featuring 12-foot-thick stone walls that may once have supported a tower. Unusual structures such as this will be of great significance later in our quest.

All in all, twenty-two significant markers, both man-made and natural, form the construction of the Orkney triangle, so if this is all a coincidence, it is very convincing.

Since the ancients were fond of mirroring things, I wondered what might unfold if the triangle were projected downwards.

Ironically the tip opposite the partly eroded Point of Cott mound is itself halfway into the sea at the southern shore of the island of Hoy. If a structure ever existed here, it has already succumbed to erosion. Northwards from this tip, the west arm passes the high ridge marking the exact geodetic center of Hoy, from which it is just possible to see Vestra Fiold. It skirts the Dwarfie Stane, passes through a *broch* beside the beach, makes landfall on Orkney at the artificially terraformed citadel of Stromness, continues, passes through a mound and finishes at Vestra Fiold.

The construction lines pass though various mounds, and no less than six strategic summits, including that of the highest hill on Orkney. Notably, the southeast construction line bisects the Bookan-Stenness alignment beside the Comet Stone and the Ring of Brodgar, implying the location of the stone circles was originally factored into this geometric blueprint.

Finally, the eastern arm from Hoy to Head of Work is relatively uneventful, since much of the trajectory is now the drowned bay of Scapa Flow. When it finally makes landfall, it advances through the sprawl of Orkney's main town, Kirkwall. Predictably, the relentless expansion of human population has left little room for the past. That said, a few hundred yards west of the arm stand the old law courts, palaces, and the imposing cathedral of Kirkwall, perhaps the holiest sanctuary in the northern isles, in whose vicinity once stood the *Thingvellir*, a field featuring a prehistoric mound from which citizens were allowed the freedom to air and settle outstanding grievances, form policy, refine outdated laws, sentence criminals, settle questions of blood-money (payable in cases of murder), pass legislation and arrange marriages. In time these focal points of open-air democracy became known as parliaments. The main gathering took place at midsummer, drawing people from every corner of the archipelago and culminating with a recital of the entire corpus of sacred teaching and tradition, from memory, by the wisdom keeper. This prodigious effort would take an entire day, for which the hoarse individual was given a well-deserved standing ovation.

Finding the exact location of the *Thingvellir* is another matter. Early historians such as Samuel Hibbert identify the stones of Stenness as the original place of assembly,[4] just as I had intuited when visiting the site. It is not unreasonable to suggest that the importance of Stenness waned with the passing of time and the practical needs of an emerging society, and by the 9th century Kirkwall had taken over the role of civic, legal and ceremonial center, with the national *Thing* convening here under the tutelage of Norwegian chieftains Jarl Rognvald and Jarl Erlend Haraldsson (incidentally the root of the title 'Earl'). Gatherings are said to have taken place on a green to the east of the cathedral.[5] The location would not have been chosen haphazardly, but most likely from a precedent established in remote times. The archipelago's polar axis has been calculated to pass through the high ground a few hundred yards east of the cathedral, essentially marking the geodetic center of Orkney,[6] and the location also coincides with the trajectory of the Orkney triangle. Thus the Kirkwall *Thingvellir* formed part of this design, a sacred center in its own right.

The process of determining the sacred center was of great benefit to early communities as a whole. When Celtic monks moved north to Iceland, to be joined there by Norwegians escaping the centralized rule of Harald Fairhair around 874 AD, the Scandinavian migrants brought ancient rituals to this most northern of abodes. This included the pillars of the high seat from their ancestral temple, which they proceeded to strategically place around Iceland according to a predetermined foundation plan: a geodetic code, drawn up from a remote era, blending sacred geometry, geodesy, astronomy and symbolic number to establish a divine order across the land. Rocks,

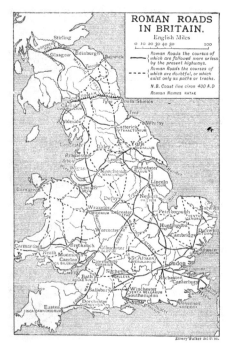

rivers, hills and other notable elements in the landscape fell under a kind of mythical spell. By establishing hallowed ground across Iceland, a foundation was provided for the people to live according to the laws of divine harmony, leading, in theory, to a balanced society. [7] What is worthy of note is that much of the information for this enterprise was coded within the *Sagas*, through allegory, symbolism and mathematics, based on knowledge handed down from a remote time of gods.[8]

Tenth century Iceland was divided into four quarters, united at its geodetic center by the national assembly, the *Al-thing*. To locate it, the lawgiver Ulfljotur commissioned his brother, Grimur Geitskor, who spent a year walking the length and breadth of Iceland, surveying and measuring from hills, mountains and promontories, for which every household rewarded him with one penny apiece.

Since this civilization has moved progressively northwards, the rules of a divinely ordered landscape would have been applied earlier on Orkney. If we assume that Orkney's sacred sites are the earliest in Britain – the notable exception being the three original post holes at Stonehenge, radiocarbon dated to between 7000-8000 BC [9] and, incidentally, mirroring the belt of Orion on the winter solstice c.6800 BC – the mysterious surveyors also took their method south to Ireland, where the same geodetic rules were applied, and to England, with its conical mounds and sacred centers laid out according to an orderly mathematical matrix across wide, rolling landscapes.[10]

Similar feats of engineering are seen in Britain's network of ancient roads. Welsh kings remarked on the ruler-straight tracks crisscrossing Britain, old beyond memory by their time, to the point where no one had an inkling as to who built them. Universities may still dole out the tired old line that Romans were responsible for this network, yet it was known among the Romans themselves that the roads were already indescribably old by the time their soldiers used them as convenient routes by which to speedily conquer much of Europe. When the Romans arrived in Britain, they found the same system already in place linking the ancient cult centers, from which arose the oldest cities. And if the Romans *did* build them, then it is odd how Ireland should have exactly the same system in place despite it never having been colonized by the Romans. Modern excavations show the tracks to be of prehistoric origin, repaired and resurfaced by the Romans, and what's more, the originals are as well levelled and drained as the 'modern' repairs.

Many of the tracks across England and Ireland are so straight that no deviation from the line is detectable — an astonishing feat for anyone, especially as it is far easier to make roads bend to natural contours and obstacles impeding their path. Since they also reference or are closely linked to prehistoric monuments, the roads, temples, mounds and stone circles must have formed part of a harmonious but now forgotten geodetic system.

When the Romans pushed into Persia they found the same long, straight tracks still in operation, allowing them to easily reach the sacred center of every district. Indeed, Persia is the region where most of these straight tracks survive – a legacy from an original root culture. The same situation played out with the Spanish in South America, who made good use of the fine paved roads connecting sacred and administrative centers across the Andes. These were attributed to the Inca, except that older cultures such as the Puquina and Aymara, who precede the Inca by over 8000 years, speak of thousands of miles of tracks made by extraordinary people from a time long forgotten. Likewise, Celtic traditions are replete with references to great men and giants

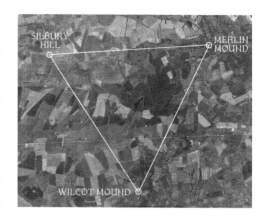

of the remote past whose works were eventually left to decay. Perhaps the surveyors of Orkney belonged to the same class of world academy.

The Orkney triangle was repeated two thousand years later in southern Britain. Adjacent to the world's largest stone circle at Avebury, Europe's largest conical mound Silbury forms a perfect equilateral triangle with its two counterparts, Merlin's Mound, and the now destroyed Wilcot mound. When mirrored, the tip touches a fourth mound at Barbury Castle to the north.[11] The same blueprint was used to mark London's original parliament mounds, allegedly constructed by groups of people arriving from northern Greece.[12]

All that is known about these gifted cosmic surveyors reaches us in fragments, through folklore or the Icelandic *Sagas*. It is estimated that Scandinavians arrived in Orkney in the 8th century – too late in our particular adventure – but they mention two types of people long established there, each distinct from the other. There were the Peti, a small people with "strange habits,"[13] considered to have been the original settlers and known to early historians, who named the region *Terra Petorum*.[14]

The other group, the Papae, were more distinguished and wore white robes,[15] the kind of garment typically worn in ancient cultures to identify priests and sages

– a practice also ascribed 11,000 years ago to the flood gods, who were attributed with the same demeanor.[16] Certainly the Papae of Orkney were important enough to lend their name to the furthest flung island in the archipelago, Papa Westray, home to a variety

of religious buildings, including the best-preserved ancient house in northern Europe, estimated to have been in use by 3500 BC.[17]

Since they spoke an entirely different language, the Papae were not only engaged in a separate profession, they may have been of a different race altogether. Scandinavian historians believed they arrived in Orkney via Norway, and if so their physiognomy may also have been different.

Both the Papae and the Peti are associated with abodes of a sacred nature. Perhaps one group mapped the sky while the other attended to stonemasonry and monuments, anchoring the calculations to the land. Such a division of roles was common in the temple raising practices of ancient Egypt,[18] and an examination of these people's etymological fingerprint reveals a definite intertwinement. Access to the Egyptian temple was restricted to the learned, the purified and the initiated, qualities reflected in their white robes of office, and the nickname *petriu*, 'those who see', visionaries, initiates with more finely attuned faculties, precisely the kind of responsible individuals one wants in charge of a sacred environment. The related term *petiu* is even closer to the Scottish name. It means 'heavenly beings', while the derivative *petr* means 'a region of sky',[19] so clearly the *petriu* or *petiu*, and by extension the Peti, were involved with understanding the stars and their shamanic potential. Elegant and puissant, they were referred to by the Persians as *peri*, whom they described as tall and graceful people possessing the gifts of clairvoyance and the ability to walk between worlds.

The Persian description is somewhat at odds with that of the Peti of Orkney as "small people," however, it ought to be remembered that the accounts by the Scandinavians were preceded by those of Christian monks who'd migrated from Ireland, where they had already established a precedent in miniaturizing the ancient priesthood of that land in order to elevate their own, so it is quite feasible that the source of the Scandinavian stories was corrupted, or at the very least, biased. We shall examine this later.

The name Papae, on the other hand, may be a corruption of *p'apegh*, the Armenian term for a monk or holy person. Its diminutive *pap* denotes 'a grandfather or elder', while the extension *papenakan* means 'inherited from ancestors'.

If the picture painted here is correct then we are presented in Orkney with a priestly class possessing an ancient inherited knowledge handed down from an established yet remote culture, and as early chroniclers correctly noted, they were not local. As from where these strangers might have originated, on the basis of modern population samples, one genetic group migrated from the Balkans via eastern Scotland,[20] while Y-chromosomal evidence suggests a second group migrated between 13,000-3000 BC from Iberia to the western and southern British Isles, contributing 24% of modern genetic lines.[21] But perhaps the most telling study concerns the DNA of Scotland's highly diverse people, which pinpoints their origins in Siberia, Arabia and Egypt.[22]

A calendar stone from Westray, near Point of Cott.
Note the similarity to the one from Tarxien temple, Malta,
also used to mark the solstices and equinoxes.

Cnoc Ceann a Gharraidh
watches over a pilgrim.

6

ISLES OF BRIDES

hey say if you don't like the weather in the Outer Hebrides wait fifteen minutes. I waited. It changed. I was pleased. The sheep grazing around me didn't care one way or the other, forever looking downwards at yet another mesmerizing blade of grass.

I recall seeing my first photo of a stone circle on the Isle of Lewis decades ago. It looked all too familiar. I knew immediately I had to travel here someday. Now I return almost every year, another name on my growing list of 'second homes'.

In order to understand what took place on Orkney one needs to look at the region as a whole rather than the fragmented political and geographical atlas it is today, which includes Ireland.

The fifteen inhabited and fifty uninhabited islands that make up the Outer Hebrides – the most prominent being Benbecula, North and South Uist, Harris and Lewis – feature some of the most dramatic landscapes in Scotland. The serrated peaks of Harris resemble Shangri-La or Mordor depending on the mood swing of weather.

They give way to nearly eight thousand freshwater lochs, treeless moors, *machair* (low-lying dune pastureland) and blanket peat bog on Lewis. Europe's most pristine sandy beaches are found here too, a warm Gulf Stream making them friendly to skinny dippers, so long as they're unaware of the weather: during gales, the courtyard of Barra Head lighthouse fills with seawater despite it being on a cliff 600 feet above the sea.

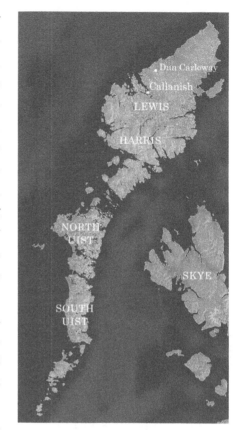

Like Orkney, much of the archipelago is a drowned coastline with deeply indented lochs. Prior to the 15-foot rise in sea level that took place between 3200-2700 BC, this was a formidable landmass in the middle of the Atlantic. Even now Harris and Lewis combined form the third largest island after Britain and Ireland, a 130-mile chunk of some of the oldest rocks on Earth, such as metamorphic Lewisian gneiss, forced by pressure from the Earth's core 3 billion years ago, its dramatic journey recorded by undulating veins of feldspar, mica, hornblende and quartz. When lit by the low light of dawn and sunset it reveals a palette of cream, yellow, gold, pink, red, grey and black, especially erotic when the stone is wet, with sparkles of light winking at the passing visitor. It is the most visually striking of any stone, the high point of the God of Nature as a geologist.

Of forty-two known chambered cairns in the region, half exist in a good state of preservation on North Uist alone. Sig More is one such monument, now partly submerged at high tide, proving such structures long pre-date the official timeframe. In fact there is evidence of human activity throughout the Hebrides as early as 8000 BC.[1] Two thousand years later the climate became warmer and hospitable, with islands supporting a considerable population sharing a balanced relationship with a lean yet productive landscape. But around 2500 BC severe climate change strained agricultural production, and further inclement conditions in 1500 BC forced a mass depopulation to mainland Scotland. The islands were abandoned, the land became fallow, and peat invaded every crag, covering monuments with a blanket of decaying plant matter by as much as six feet. Stone circles and passage mounds literally went underground.

Still, the peat, combined with extreme environmental forces and socio-economic conditions, have helped preserve some of Britain's most complete stone circles. And compared to what little is known about the monuments of Orkney, even less is known about those of the Outer Hebrides, which makes this quest so much more delicious.

The name Hebrides is a corruption of Hy Bridhe, the Isles of Brides – a possible commemoration of the Gaelic goddess Bridhe, otherwise known as Bridgit.[2] A second, and equally compelling interpretation rests on the movement of language, with Gaelic having evolved from Indo-European regions, specifically Asia Minor, with elements of Egyptian language. Earlier I brought up the possibility of an Armenian connection in Scottish sacred language. I would like to add to this a people who existed long before 1200 BC, the Bryges, who upon migrating from Armenia to Asia Minor became known as Phrygians. Confusingly, as they continued into western

73

Europe they took back their original name.[3] The root *bryge* is speculated to be an Indo-European word for 'mountain', but semantically it is applied to an elevated or illustrious class, a people of noble origin.[4] *Hy*, on the other hand, is a contraction of *hye*, a person of Armenian origin, which itself derives from *hayk*, the constellation Orion. Thus to a visitor from Armenia, the Hye Bryges ostensibly means 'domain of noble people of Orion'.

A third working possibility lies with the numerous religious sects that, for as long as anyone can recall, have made the Hebrides their home, seeking solitude or refuge from persecution. In their sacred teachings, the highest level of initiation was marked by a candidate symbolically marrying a divine bride, whereupon he or she becomes a single entity, neither masculine nor feminine but whole. During this ceremony, performed inside restricted chambers, sacred caves or closed vessels, a poison was administered to render initiates comatose while they traveled to an allegorical land in the west. Insofar as northern Europe is concerned, one cannot travel further west than the Outer Hebrides. From this point of view, then, the name 'Isles of the Brides' was given in homage of individuals practicing a longstanding spiritual tradition with roots in the Middle East, India and Japan.[5]

Combining these possibilities with the Gaelic name for the islands, *Innse Gall* (Islands of the Strangers), we are offered a picture of people migrating here from elsewhere with special abilities and, as in Orkney, possibly of contrasting physiognomy to the general inhabitants. Indeed it is said that the Isle of Lewis itself was populated in a remote time by a race of giants known as Formori, who were also present in Ireland. It seems the Hebrides are a kaleidoscope of fragments and whispers of unusual inhabitants. Perhaps their monuments might add more meat to the bone.

There is but one main road to the west of Lewis. Along the way, dozens of stone circles and standing stones lie among the moors, alone, rarely visited, for the most part recumbent or obstructed by dense peat bog. Giants and other unusual people also make their mark on this landscape, at least in name: Loch an Druidhe (Lake of the Druids), Sithean Mor (Hill of the Shining Ones), Tom a Mhorair (Cave of the Giant). As idyllic as these places sound they are difficult to reach, protected by deep bog, mud and hundreds of small lochs, and in the summer by that relentless bloodsucker of the glen, the midge.

I continued on to the opposite coast to examine Scotland's single largest standing stone.

Clach an Trushal seems underwhelming from a distance, until you walk within its shadow. Only then does its 15-foot girth and 19-foot height above the soil remind you of what our ancestors were capable of accomplishing. In the adjacent field wall, pieces of its twin lie interwoven with stones borrowed from the beach. An attendant stone circle once stood on a flat earthen platform beyond. Given the size of its sockets, the megaliths must have been equally formidable, but in the 19th century they attracted the wrong sort of people and were shattered by fire and cold water. The monument lost its sacred employment to become building material. The obligatory passing of time and custom on this land are seldom courteous to the past. That's why there's peat. The gods never really left – they merely resurrected as decaying plant matter to protect a project whose intention was to outlive eternity.

A few minutes south, sited on a gentle promontory surrounded by lochs, stands the village of Callanish, hub of nine known stone circles. Visible on a ridge to the east is the unpronounceable Cnoc Ceann a Gharraidh, followed a short walk away by the unspellable Cnoc Fillibhir Bheag. Three more lie to the north in various stages of dishevelment, one having been entirely stripped of stone for housing. To the southeast, on the summit of a tall hill, is Cu'l a' Chleit.

Ten minutes away on the only road south is a stone circle that practically all visitors miss, because Ceann Hulavig lies just over the brow of a hill. Five of its original nine monoliths remain upright, covered in green hoary lichen and regularly ankle deep in water, thanks to the removal of peat during excavations in 1846 that gives the intruding rainfall little chance of escape. Composed of gneiss laced with ripples of feldspar and spatters of mica, the stones are electrifying as much as they are magnetizing, and it is always difficult to depart from here.

Ceann Hulavig may be the smallest of the low-lying circles but it is certainly the most potent. There is a presence here of learning, of spiritual know-how, as

Clach an Truishal. A small stone.

though one is standing among an assembly of people in charge of ancestral wisdom. It is a feeling shared by most who care to venture here. Despite a mesmerizing view of the rolling plains, like others of its kind Ceann Hulavig was not placed on the summit of the hill, as would seem practical. Instead it is placed geodetically so that when observed from Callanish, Sirius and Orion could be seen at their mid-heaven positions in 3000 BC, along with the winter solstice sunrise. Conversely, from Ceann Hulavig the summer solstice Sun was seen setting over Callanish.

Taken as a whole, the stone circles, with their unique vistas and mechanical referencing to specific landmarks, all converge on the slowly ascending ridge upon which stand the cruciform stone rows and circle of Callanish itself, the queen bee surrounded by her hive. With stones up to 19.5 feet tall, Callanish and its sisters form a practical and existential whole, a Neolithic drama set amid another engineered landscape.

With Loch Roag for a backdrop, it is easy to imagine Neolithic people arriving here by boat from the Atlantic. Its western approach follows a narrow

The magical Ceann Hulavig.

Cleitir.

waterway beyond which rises the island of Great Bernara. Forty feet up on a steep cliff stands a semi-circle of stones named Cleitir, after the Gaelic term for 'cliff'. It is odd that anyone should erect 9-foot tall stones on such an awkward incline when level ground, not to mention the expansive view that comes with it, is freely available a mere eighty feet further uphill. Either the builders aligned the semi-circle to a specific feature to justify the inconvenient placement – and indeed it does mark the southernmost Lunar set as well as the Beltane sunrise – or a telluric current must flow here (it does). Perhaps these reasons are sufficient. However, across the shore a lone tall stone seems separated from the others, dragged 300 feet to its present position when rising seas widened the waterway between the two islands, so the remainder of an original circle could feasibly lie underwater.[6]

If so, Cleitir may have served a dramatic purpose in its heyday. Visitors arriving by ship would have passed within a breath of the stone circle, paying homage and using the moment to ritually prepare prior to entering the sacred space around Callanish, as was the custom in other parts of the world. A pier where pilgrims disembarked is known to have existed at the foot of the Callanish headland, giving rise to another name by which the site was known, Kallaöarnes, 'the port or landing place of Öarnes'. Who was this visitor, and what lofty office did he or she occupy to merit the memorializing of the name?

The modern pilgrim to Callanish arrives less theatrically, by road, and is first treated to the stone circle Cnoc Fillibhir Bheag, a series of ellipses consisting of 13 monoliths, beloved of a local herd of highland cattle as scratching posts. No experience compares with that of meditating here while sharing your stone with a large, shaggy orange-haired, big-horned bovine. The stones are sumptuous, rich in feldspar, gneiss and quartz, with tips deliberately shaped to reference the contours of the southerly mountain range. Collectively they are situated on the tail of a crag where festivities took place to commemorate the Celtic feast of Beltane, whose sunrise was marked here c.5000 BC.

Seen from here, the outline of the long stone avenue of Callanish resembles a procession of monks making their way towards the circle at the head of the promontory.

Cnoc Fillibhir Bheag.

A short walk across a patch of unforgiving bog leads you to Cnoc Ceann a' Gharraidh, once an ellipse of 18, possibly 19 stones of which only 5 now remain, one being an impressive 12-foot tall triangle. The numbers suggest the site was used to calibrate the solar and lunar calendars every 18.6 years. Its known alignments mark the southernmost moonrise as well as the winter solstice, as observed from Callanish.

While each stone circle acts independently as an observatory and ceremonial site in its own right, collectively they function as fore- and back-sights for the measuring of stellar objects from Callanish, making every monument on this landscape interrelated and interdependent. Clearly someone long ago possessed an accumulated understanding of complex geodetic work.

During his tour of the Western Isles in 1695, Martin Martins recorded villagers' folklore. Callanish in particular was said to have been a meeting place for Druidhe priests at significant times of the year when villagers would gather to hear them; Loch an Druidhe, less than two miles away, still commemorates their presence. The stones were understood to be meeting places of stellar and earthly currents from which the people benefited, thus the circles were cared for and protected. One tale from a time of extreme famine on Lewis tells of a mother who walked down to the sea to take her life – one less mouth to feed to save the rest of the family. But before she could follow through, a white cow with red eyes came out of the waves and told her to ask the villagers to bring pails for the cow to fill with milk. The villagers didn't believe the woman, let alone a cow providing sustenance for an entire village, but when they saw the cow among the stones they changed their minds and everyone lived happily ever after – until an evil woman cast a spell to send the people back to poverty. She greedily took two pails to fill for herself but the cow refused to give her as much as a drop. The next day she approached the cow with one pail whose bottom she'd replaced with a sieve. She milked the cow relentlessly until it ran dry, and contented, took her malice and left the stone circle. The following day the village women gathered at the stones with their pails but the cow was never seen again.

This simple allegorical tale makes a clear association between respect for places of veneration and the protection they afford, as an unbroken circle of sustenance is established through a meeting between the material plane and the Otherworld. Aside from marking the movement of the heavens and acting as places of council, stone circles were regarded as insurance policies. Predictably, the advent of Christianity brought about their destruction, but despite warnings and curses from local priests, as late as the 18th century people would sneak away to visit

Callanish reclaimed from the peat in 1859.

the stones, specially at Beltane and the summer solstice, to ensure the temples were not neglected.

Thankfully Callanish was spared such humiliation. By 1000 BC the site was fully abandoned, half of the stones gradually obscured by six feet of peat, and only through its periodic removal for heating fuel did villagers become aware in 1857 of the true scale of the monument in their midst. Such was the peat cover that archaeologists mistook some stones as fallen when in fact they were looking at their tips.

Another folk tale reveals a crucial piece of information as to who may originally have been responsible for Callanish and its attendant sites. As with megalithic sacred places along the coasts of Brittany, Ireland and Britain, the stories describe how the stones were erected by a priestly race of tall people or giants who arrived with a group of black men or people of comparatively darker complexion. Callanish served as a meeting place for their council, but when they resisted encroaching religion a Christian saint allegedly turned them all to stone.

Such tales are an admixture of tradition and mnemonic symbolism overwritten with Christian propaganda, since they long pre-date the actions of posthumously rewarded saints. Hundreds of surviving accounts throughout the world record a similar outcome between tall people and stones, indicating that the megaliths themselves came to possess the memory and intent of those who originally placed them on the land like vertical libraries. This is not as far-fetched as it may seem. Monitored experiments show that when intent is properly guided it sends a packet of electromagnetic data capable of interacting with crystalline forms, such as the silica on the memory board of a computer.[7] Since standing stones were chosen for their silica content, this piezoelectric substance is capable of being similarly imprinted by anyone with the correct training. Conversely, a visitor in the right state of awareness is able to access the information placed there by ancient practitioners, just as people in a state of meditation still do at Ceann Hulavig, myself included.

The avenue of stones leading to the Callanish stone circle follows a northeast trajectory, a direction that symbolically, and sometimes literally, aligns to the summer solstice, the time of the year when the light of the Sun is at its most prominent. This pinnacle of illumination also equates with ancestral wisdom, thus the avenue once served as a processional route for wisdom keepers, just as at Stonehenge, Luxor, and the original mound beneath Chartres cathedral, whose alignments all follow the same trajectory. The avenue leading to Callanish originally began a mile away at a chambered cairn, now partly ruined beside the village road; a path of slabs aligned to the northeast once led to the chamber itself, while the entrance faced the stone circle. Much of the avenue has since been inundated by the expanding loch due to rising seas; other stones were removed for building material and some still lie buried in villagers' gardens.

Two shorter stone rows traverse the top of the ridge, meeting the circle from east and west, giving the

site its cruciform appearance. A considerable period after the site was completed, a chambered cairn used for initiation was added.[8]

Composed of gneiss, quartz and hornblende, the circle of thirteen slender stones numerically references the cycle of the Moon. The local husband and wife team of Gerald and Margaret Ponting spent a decade observing how Callanish is placed at the ideal latitude from which to mark the Moon's most southerly position, and how every 18.6 years it rises out of the belly of Cailleach na Mointeach (Old Woman of the Moors), the mountain range forming the southern horizon. The lunar orb barely skims across her sleeping body, setting shortly after into the vessel that is the Clisham range to the west. When observed from the avenue of stones, the Moon makes a spectacular sight as it descends behind a natural outcrop beyond the circle, only to reappear beside the central and tallest monolith – a thin and sinuous piece of gneiss measuring 19.6 feet, coincidentally the same height of the stones of Stenness, and similar in appearance. Other stones shapes bear close resemblance to those of the Ring of Brodgar, and yet others on the island of Arran, despite the sites being composed of different geology,[9] opening up the possibility that the shapes were not chosen randomly for their aesthetic alone but to fulfil a purpose as yet unknown. One of most visually striking stones on the avenue, with a slanted top and a curve like a bulbous finger, is near-identical to one found 500 miles away on the avenue leading to Avebury.

The Callanish stones also indicate the horizon position of the rising Moon at the northern extreme of the Major Lunar Standstill. On this occasion it is seen setting into the distant stone circle Ceann Hulavig. Altogether, Margaret and Gerald's admirable surveys show 342 possible astronomical sightlines between nineteen local sites, with 220 being intervisible, demonstrating the ancient architects' recurring precision on the land and their acute knowledge of the sky.[10]

Moon as seen over the Clisham range, setting into the circle.

The placement of Callanish on its imposing ridge is a well-reasoned fusion of human, landscape and celestial considerations to achieve a coherent whole, so much so that word of this magical landscape spread far and wide. Even in 55 BC, Diadorus of Sicily was talking up the Isle of Lewis and its astronomical associations: "There is also on the island a notable temple which is spherical in shape...the Moon as viewed from this island appears but a little distance from earth... the god visits every 19 years."

These relationships between sky and ground are not observable from any other position, thus the ancient astronomers took great pains to survey the landscape prior to establishing their temples on sites that are also outstanding geological features in themselves. And just to make it harder, they chose to place their creations on crag-and-tail glacial formations with axes running north to south. From the air they resemble teardrops or the paths of descending comets.[11]

It is therefore odd that amid such meticulous calculation they chose to place Callanish where a prominent crag by the name of Cnoc an Tursa blocks an otherwise uninterrupted 360-degree view of the horizon. Looking at Callanish from afar, it becomes clear that the circle and its central monolith are deliberately using the mound-shaped crag. An archaeological excavation of Cnoc an Tursa indeed found sockets for the missing stones of the avenue, along with a large backfilled pit, potentially a socket for a stone whose scale would have created a focal point in itself. What's more, the dig uncovered a long history of replacement, suggesting the stone may have fallen or, like so many others, was felled and used for building material then replaced by people striving to maintain the site.[12] Taken as a whole, Cnoc an Tursa and its fissured entrance form a constituent part of Callanish, in effect creating a symbolic gate between the terrestrial stone circle and whatever object is meant to be seen rising

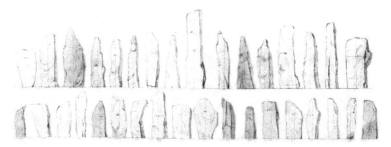

Shapes of Callanish stones recur at other sites.

86

beyond the outcrop, to be observed only from within the circle itself.

A relationship between sky and land may not have been the only consideration for ancient architects. As a group, the Callanish stone circles cluster within an extremely strong gravity anomaly zone, while the locations of the circles themselves delineate a localized region of low natural magnetism.[13] A similar interaction is at play in Orkney. The Ring of Brodgar sits on a fault line, while Stenness is located precisely at the branching of two fault lines. One is instantly reminded of the sites in Brittany, where the densest distribution of standing stones in all of France coincides with the country's most active geological faults. In essence, the quartz-rich stones are in a permanent state of subtle vibration that in turn generates a piezoelectric effect.[14] This follows a distinct pattern throughout the world of sacred sites having been strategically located to take advantage of such anomalies, the idea being to influence a visitor's state of consciousness. The stones themselves were carefully considered to amplify these relationships, hence the reason why they were often sourced far from their intended locations. The stones at Callanish, for example, contain a fair amount of hornblende, a silicate of iron, transforming them into lighting rods that attract electric and magnetic currents to the site.

During my first visit I stayed with a farming family who live minutes away from the stones, enabling me to spend every waking minute, even a few in the middle of the night, walking Callanish and making additional calculations. Since I am also a photographer and the owner shared my obsession, he generously arranged to leave my dinner in the oven every evening. It seems that the rain generally stops and the clouds part around fifteen minutes before the Sun sets, providing a narrow but excellent window when the light upon the stones is at its most dramatic. Or in photographic parlance, you'll be late for dinner every evening.

He was not wrong. I was also able to have more time to look into the anomaly that is Cnoc an Tursa and why it spoils an otherwise perfect view. After taking the necessary alignments, I wandered the site for the umpteenth time – it is next to impossible to leave here – and allowed the spirit of place to share what I ought to know. At this point I recalled the stone circles of Orkney and how they mirror the first rising of Orion's Belt on the winter solstice c.5300 BC. No such association has ever been explored at Callanish, but if made it would establish a coherent pattern of behavior by the elusive architects.

Standing inside the circle, looking down the southerly row of stones towards Cnoc an Tursa, Orion's Belt rose for the first time above the crag on the winter solstice c.5000 BC. The spirit of place was communicating well. But there was one more surprise. At the same moment, looking back at the opposite end of the avenue, which aligns to the

Orion's Belt rising over Cnoc an Tursa, framed within Callanish.

celestial pole, the bright star Lyra appeared above the stones. Oddly enough, the same dual relationship presents itself at another striking ancient monument 2500 miles away in the region that used to be ancient Armenia – the enigmatic Stone Circle D at Göbekli Tepe – the difference is that it took place there five-and-a-half thousand years earlier.[15]

A common theme now presents itself between Orkney and the Outer Hebrides. We have a group of master astronomers and seafarers erecting memorable structures; along with the Sun and Moon, they are obsessed with Orion; they are unusually tall and wear white tunics; they are possessed of an artistic sensitivity; and they are expert surveyors for whom the arranging of monuments on undulating and challenging terrain was not an impediment. Using archaeoastronomy as one reliable method for dating their work, we can surmise that having established themselves on Orkney around 5300 BC, these itinerant architects sailed south within 300 years and expanded their cosmic enterprise. If so, they were present at Callanish almost two thousand years prior to the earliest human activity unearthed so far,[16] but with so much of Lewis still hidden by peat, who knows what supporting evidence a lucky turn of a spade may yet reveal.

Be that as it may, the most unusual monument in this region is neither a megalith nor a stone circle. A few miles north of Callanish stands a tapered stone tower at Dun Carloway that, like others of its kind, has vexed historians for centuries because these iconic structures are unique to Orkney, Shetland, the Western Isles and the tip of northern Scotland. To quote one: "It means that we have here the remains of a period of architectural activity which has no parallel in the early history of our country."[17]

Dun Carloway has been used, reused and adapted over time, but even in its dilapidated state it is the best preserved of them all. It is built of well-fitted stone without mortar. The central courtyard is surrounded by a hollow wall, inside which a staircase winds its way to where there used to be upper galleries. From what remains of the structure, windows appear to have been sparse.

The tower incorporates features far and beyond what is necessary in a residence. For example, the design is based on music ratios: its external to internal diameter conforms to the octave; the wall from north to south varies in thickness by Pi; the main door is framed to a ratio of 1.33:1, equivalent to the note F. It's as though the residence was intended for a musician or a mathematician.

Or an observer of the sky perhaps? The entrance is impractically placed to face the most windswept direction off the ocean, yet faces a pointed rock ledge which references the Minor Lunar Standstill as well as the Crossquarters – the midpoints between solstices and equinoxes that mark the beginning of seasons in the Celtic calendar. All this specialist information seems out-of-place and far beyond the everyday requirements of eating and sleeping in what is officially touted as the residence of a noble family. There is evidence of people living here in 100 BC, but if the tower was meant to offer long-term protection from raiders (the other explanation),

the fact that it could shelter no more than a dozen people and animals comfortably, and had no access to a well or sewage disposal, means that two weeks of siege by half a dozen pirates was all the effort required before the besieged began to look at urine as fine wine or to each other as a source of nourishment. There is also the problem of the tower standing fifty feet lower than the adjacent bedrock. As any military strategist knows, if you don't own the high ground the outcome will not be positive. Perhaps the tower, like the ancient monuments around it, was inherited from an earlier period and re-used by different people with different needs?

The bardic traditions of the region are more accommodating: they tell of a time when such buildings were associated with a race of giants. Those tall people once more, "certain strangers," people from afar. Whatever its origin and purpose, one thing is clear: three hundred and seventy *duns* are known to exist throughout the Scottish Isles.[18] They have no architectural parallel in the history of this region. They are individual and strangely out of place, an anomaly confined to Scotland.

Or are they?

Dun Carloway. And as it appeared in 1890.

A walk under an island. MacKinnon's Cave.

7

A TRADITION OF
SACREDNESS

id ya just arrive frum da menlaand on daat big boat?" enquired the old gentleman.

"On the ferry? Yes, I did. Why?" I replied.

"Gud. Then yell be gettin' back on it laterrr!"

This warm welcome in the small village store of Craignure made my arrival on the isle of Mull official. Island people in this weather-beaten part of the globe tend to be insular and private, and having gotten to know a few in my time, including the police, with the exception of one grumpy old codger I'd trust them with my life.

An ample stock of Stochan's Thick Oat Cakes is paramount to survival when walking into the wilds of the Inner Hebrides, a collection of seventy-nine islands brushing the coastline of western Scotland like pebbles of a drowned land, of which Mull is the largest. Armed with these triangular biscuits you will discover the source of Tolkien's inspiration for Lembas bread, because one piece is all it takes to satisfy your stomach for the rest of the day. If it was good enough for Hobbits to make it to Mordor, it's good enough for me on Mull.

I came to walk the wilderness because it satisfies

my craving for solitude and melancholy. Even when the rain falls there is a peace like no other. The shimmer of water on the aged rock releases an aroma, a language of knowing, of spiritual truth whispered by souls from bygone ages who came here seeking answers to the past and have patiently waited among the heather for a curious person with whom to share what they found.

Indeed Mull is a focal point from which to gain perspective on the long traditions of sacredness and religious tolerance that are central to the history of the Western Isles. Although our quest so far has taken place around 5000 BC, the knowledge introduced by the elusive architects of the stones influenced people and priesthoods well into the historical era. Megaliths were the memory sticks of their day, each suffused with vital information, emitting a signal to draw the curious, the spiritual and the wise, and from here they promulgated the knowledge to those who had ears to hear, and did so free from fear of persecution.

One group to heed the call was the Culdee, an early Christian sect, in every positive connotation, who traveled through Europe to settle in France, Ireland and northern Wales, and from there to Scotland where, two thousand years ago, they established religious sites on earlier pagan places of veneration. Support for dating this apostolic mission to Britain comes from the erudite Bishop Ussher, who wrote: "The British National Church was founded AD 36, 160 years before heathen Rome confessed Christianity,"[1] to which the ecclesiastical historian Eusebius of Caesarea added: "the Apostles passed beyond the ocean to the isles called the Britannic Isles." The Gaels referred to them as *Keledei*, 'children of God', but the term is predated by the Chaldean *Culdich*, meaning 'strangers from a distance,' and may well support a statement by Freculphus, bishop of Lisieux, that friends and disciples of Jesus – a company that originally included Joseph of Aramathea, Lazarus, Mary, Martha, Marcella and Maximin – found refuge in Britain following their persecution, coming at the invitation of high-ranking Druidhe officials.[2]

The root of *culdich* is *khaldi,* the ancient Armenian Supreme God, at a stroke proving these peripatetic monks were both 'children of God' as well as 'strangers from a distance'. Their early presence is found in the Scottish village of Feart-nan-Gall (now anglicized as Fortingall), the 'stronghold of the strangers'.[3] The area was already an established Neolithic sacred site featuring dolmens, extensive rock art and stone circles, at the heart of which stands a yew tree whose girth once measured fifty-two feet and is estimated to be around 2000 years old, making it consistent with the arrival of the strangers from afar.[4]

The Culdee chose to live like hermits in caves or man-made cells resembling beehives, much like those found throughout the Near East, Macedonia, and Mediterranean islands such as Sardinia. Once they reached the Western Isles, these humble people played a crucial role in integrating the old Druidic beliefs (by then on the wane) with the eastern philosophy of the Essenes, a Gnostic Christian sect whose manner, beliefs and wardrobe the Culdee so faithfully imitated that they were alleged to be the very same Essenes who had escaped from threats to their way of life in Qumran and around the Levant. Certainly the Culdee's appearance in the Scottish isles three years after the Essenes' persecution is timely. Like the Essenes and the Druidhe, the Culdee possessed secret, sacred knowledge which they passed on to their members, they wore white robes, believed in reincarnation and an evolving soul, employed the symbol of the dove, referred to themselves as the 'sons of light' and followed the tradition of Enoch – much like an ancient group of mystics from

Asia Minor, the Tuadhe d'Anu, whose principal scribe, the antediluvian sage Enmed-Ur-anu, was the inspiration for the Biblical Enoch. But we're getting ahead of the story.

Thanks to the Culdee, the secret church of John the Baptist was able to develop in Scotland. To all intents and purposes they were the spiritual line of descent from the builders of the Temple of Solomon, and are often referred to as the 'hidden church' of Scotland, practicing their traditional spiritual life among the Western Isles, overlooked by monarchs when other monks were forced to conform to Roman Catholic practices. In the 9th century they came to the fore in public life, converting powerful people such as King Constantine of the Picts, who retired from office to become abbot of the Culdee settlement at St. Andrews. Barely two centuries later, however, under the influence of Queen Margaret, most Celtic churches were assimilated by the Church of Rome. Even so the Culdee were tolerated in areas such as Loch Leven, and as their public life faded, other groups took over the role. The Knights Hospitaller made their headquarters at Torphichen, an ancient ceremonial site dating to c.2000 BC, building their sanctuary on top of a major Culdee settlement that included ruined beehive cells once occupied by the reclusive monks in the 4th century but since fallen into decay.

All the groups listed above shared and practiced the principle of tolerance, and for them the isle of Mull became a sanctuary, just as it did for women searching for acceptance and equality, be it spiritually or in everyday pursuits. One such community was Cill-nan-noi-nighing, 'the church of the nine holy maidens', which still appears on Johan Blaeu's map of 1654 in contracted form as Kilymaig, *'church of the maiden'*. Its early predecessor was situated closer to the sea than the present church. Obviously even the women had endured enough lashings from the storms and moved inland. Still, one site that shan't be going anywhere is the adjacent hill by the name Torr-an-Ogha, the *'Hill of the Virgins'*.

On the south side of Loch na Keal there once existed a community of holy women by the name Leirnacalloch, 'Hillside of the Nuns'. Another sat along the westernmost shore of Mull, looking out across the narrow strip of water to Iona. This refuge of black nuns was called Eilean nam Ban, 'Island of Women', although to anyone who's sat for any length of time on its coarse red granite, it is pronounced more appropriately as 'island numb bum'.

Not surprisingly, the modern church avoids any reference to such places where the "weaker sex" ruled with impunity for generations. Nor does it make much of the origin of Tobar Mhoire, otherwise known as Mull's main town Tobermory, which means Well of Mary. Officially it was a watering hole dedicated to the Virgin Mary.[5]

Unofficially, but known within Scottish Rite circles, the medieval well and attendant chapel were built by fleeing Templar knights – by then rebranded as  Scottish Rite Freemasons – in tribute to their hero Mary Magdalene, the anti-establishment icon of her time.

After stopping for a dram and a fireplace – it was almost June, after all – I made my way along meandering single-lane tracks to the most reclusive part of Mull, where slow movement allows for the appreciation of a weather-beaten yet romantic landscape. A twenty-minute drive easily warps into hours. Lochbuie is where the Gulf Stream makes port, enabling this remote peninsula to be an agricultural paradise once described as the Garden of Mull. Along the southern shore of the loch, a range of hills match the path of the Milky Way on the winter solstice.

For a hard to reach location Lochbuie has drawn all manner of spiritual seekers on a quest, and that's what fascinates me about this place. In 1181 the Knights Templar dropped anchor and set up shop at Ballinacarrow in Ireland, in hindsight a fortuitous investment, because in 1307 they were forced to evacuate France in a hurry and required safe haven along the Irish coast. From there they made the short sea passage to Scotland, hugging the Western Isles to avoid detection by the English, who at the time were sympathetic to the Pope. In league with the Cistercians,[6] who pretty much followed the same doctrine and code as the Culdee, even dressed like them, the Templars pulled into Lochbuie, joined an already established community and maintained a low profile.[7]

Well, they tried. The only tall building at the head of Lochbuie is a modest keep called Moy Castle. The official story claims the cuboid structure was built in the 15th century by Hector Maclaine, a member of one of the oldest clans in Scotland. On the surface there is no reason to doubt this, except that there is no proof Hector ever built Moy castle, only that the Lochbuie estate was acquired from the Lords of the Isles at that time. As for Hector's ancestors, they had moved to Mull from Ireland back in the 13th century,[8] coincidentally around the same period the Templars were establishing footholds in both regions. A commissioned report reveals there have been a number of alterations to the tower over time, so it is quite feasible the Maclaines inherited an existing building and adapted it to their needs.[9]

As far as fortifications go, Moy Castle is oddly sited, with minimal natural defensive advantages, perched on a rock platform near the high tide mark of a pebbly beach with a narrow stream flowing on either side. Unlike the *dun* on the Isle of Lewis, the interior has ample space for provisions and living quarters, making it far more practical as a place in which to seek safety. However, there is still the issue of access to potable water during siege. It is argued that a stone shaft sunk four feet into the floor was the source of freshwater, yet a cursory examination shows this box may never have functioned as a well, partly because there is no conduit channeling the water from the adjacent streams, but mostly because the water table at this point is tainted with salt water from the tide, which would have made the besieged die of dehydration. Besides, blocking the freshwater supply would have been child's play. It is as though beneath the outer skin of Moy Castle there lurks a deeper story, and following convivial conversations on local history with Lorne Maclaine, the current clan chief of Lochbuie, I felt compelled to dig a little deeper.

Having made myself known to the new English owner of Moy Castle, who turned out to be ruder than the old codger in the village store and who, I will reveal, enjoys hoisting the Union Jack provocatively from a Scottish castle, I went back to work. As I walked around the tower, orange shafts of sunlight hustled through fast moving clouds from a passing squall, draping puddles of color upon the slopes of Ben Buie. I found it odd that, when observed from the most obvious point of approach, the sea, the tower is positioned so as not to be readily seen against the surrounding landscape. Nor do its faces, with their tiny slit windows, face the sea. Had I been a watchman on the lookout for approaching troublemakers, my job would have been formidably hampered. Here we have a landmark trying its best to remain anonymous. Such deviations from the norm reminded me of my notes on the architects of Orkney and Lewis and how they too positioned their works not where one would expect them, but where they best interacted with the sky. On a hunch I took compass measurements of the tower.

The ground plan of the tower is set at an angle no ordinary builder would employ: 51.5°, which happens to be the angle of incline of the Great Pyramid. Now, why would that have been important to Clan Maclaine? The inner brotherhood of the Templars, on the other hand, much like similar orders who practiced and implemented ancient Mysteries teachings,[10] was very much aware of this angle and its relationship to the heptagon, the central geometric figure in the rites of Scottish Freemasonry,[11] and, in turn, its numerical reference to the Egyptian goddess and patron saint of sacred buildings, Seshat. Now, why should all this be taking place on a remote site on the seaward side of a hard to reach Scottish island?

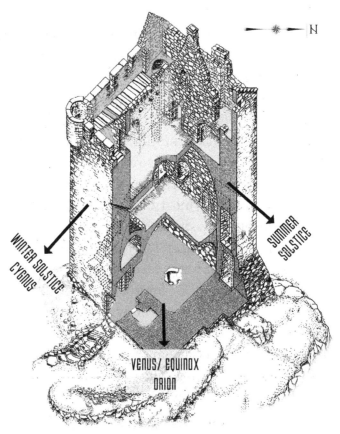

Alignments of Moy Castle.

The Templars – who, incidentally, included women – were well aware that the alignment of a building to specific objects in the sky not only bestowed it with favorable forces, it also served as a means of communication with like-minded groups following traditions outside the Church's myopic manual. To anyone in the club, so to speak, a coded building was a wink and a nod to the traveler that those residing within were people with whom one could speak freely about topics that, under the politics of the period, would have had you boiled alive. Or worse.

Out came the compass again. When allowing for the mountains framing the horizon around Lochbuie, the following calculations emerged for the 13th century: the northeast wall faces the summer solstice, the highest position of light and symbol of the attainment of wisdom. The southeast wall marks the winter solstice as well as the rising of Cygnus, constellation of the swan, symbol of the divine feminine in the era of the Templars and, in most respects, a logo of defiance against the Church. The eastern corner of the building, which is notably off by 6°, points to the rising of Venus on the spring equinox, the mark of the initiate who 'rises' after completing a secret initiation inside an underground chamber or box, much like the one in the lower section of Moy Castle, and other Templar buildings for that matter.

This same corner comes with a second reference, the rising of Orion on the winter solstice, as though the Templars were paying homage to the architects of Orkney and the Isles of the Brides.

The tide on the crescent-shaped beach was going out, inviting a long walk through a throng of straggling red-haired highland cattle, horns sharper than a spear but, on the whole, very friendly. One does not find Lochbuie by accident, I thought aloud while walking towards a lone chapel inconveniently placed on the opposite side of the bay. There would have to have been a precedent here for the teaching of ancient systems of knowledge, and if so, the Templars and others of their ilk would have known about it through the hidden grapevine. How else would anyone find this place unless through an established tradition?

And indeed there was one. Cainnech Dalåan of Ahaboe, a 6th century Celtic monk with family ties to the Druidhe and, potentially, as the corrupted family name suggests, the Tuatha dé Danann, the mythical rulers of Ireland who, like the Druidhe, were referred to as Sons of Light. Here Cainnech built a humble chapel, Caibeal Mheomhair, in the middle of nowhere, as far away from the few inhabitants of Lochbuie as one can get, and for that matter, far from every congregation on Mull. Clearly people had to work hard for their spiritual development in this place. Cainnech's chapel today bears

Caibeal Mheomhair in its remoteness.

little resemblance to the original building. The main core and sandstone font are late medieval additions from the Templar period, with the odd detail here and there reused from the earlier chapel. By 1701 it had fallen into a ruinous state and was subsequently converted into a mausoleum for the Maclaines, but this too fell into disrepair.

All this is very well, but why did an itinerant Celtic monk make it as hard as possible for a congregation to hear the words of wisdom he'd crossed a rough Irish Sea to share? As a monastic founder Cainnech well knew the value of a faithful flock and the practical need to remain financially solvent.

Perhaps the chapel itself wasn't the original attraction on this plot of land. Adjacent to the chapel grounds stands the remains of a tree circle, as though marking the space formerly occupied by a stone circle or a sacred gathering place – much like the Druidhe once did throughout southern England, and for precisely the same reason. Inside this ring, compasses fail to find north at certain times of the day and spinning pendulums go airborne in seconds, indicating a geomagnetic hotspot, a vortex of

The tree circle.

energy rising out of the ground, the kind of place upon which every sacred building is located. Such anomalies – where the laws of physics behave ever so differently on the landscape – have been sought since time immemorial by visionaries, mystics, and specifically by those engaging in shamanic travel. If a notable ancient monument once stood here to attract devout individuals like Cainnech, it may have become the stone wall now encompassing the chapel. Certainly there is an abundance of broken fieldstone lying around, but if anything of note ever existed here, no written record remains and we are none the wiser. That said, there is an ancient site of veneration still standing a few hundred yards behind Moy Castle.

After a thorough slog through shin-deep bog, one reaches the remains of a stone chamber now partly overwhelmed by the roots of trees. Given its alignment to the winter solstice it was most likely used in birthing ceremonies; in the adjacent field a lone standing stone, shielded by deep pockets of mud, asks to be appreciated. Two fields further along, behind a hawthorn hedge, the humble stone circle of Lochbuie finally comes into view.

Lochbuie stone circle. With Ben Buie watching.

They say the best things come in small packages. With respect to this circle of nine stones rising up to 6 feet out of permanent wetland, I must agree. Even with the pyramid-like presence of Ben Buie as a backdrop, it is not a photogenic site. Nor are its outliers, which act in tandem with notable features on the surrounding hills to mark the positions of the Sun and Moon. No, it's the inherent power of place that is important here, as though the circle is fulfilling an undisclosed purpose, a masterwork of such importance that its builders dressed it with anonymity. Lochbuie stone circle revels in its solitude. The last time I felt a presence like it was inside Ceann Hullavig on the Isle of Lewis.

Having paid my respects to the ancestors I sat down to write my impressions, acquiring a damp bum in the process, to the total obliviousness of the sheep grazing around me. Damp bum, numb bum... call me gentrified, but I was not prepared to acknowledge these as signs from the ancients. Time to take a break and let things sink in.

After a well-deserved hot meal of roast beef, garlic mash, lashings of thick gravy and a smidgen of vegetable, I took my notebook outside, accompanied by a wee dram of Lagavulin, the serious researcher's whisky, and an uninterrupted view of the long neck of Loch Scridain. The mirror-like water reflected the last of the evaporated rain clouds, a shaft of angular sunlight dappled the moors and mountains in a mosaic of deep oranges and reds. God playing with Its lipstick collection. The weather may be mischievous here but the sunsets are delectable.

What was going on in the seclusion of the west coast of Mull, its back turned to mainland Britain, keeping its secrets close to its chest? If ever there existed a large megalithic tradition on the island, much of it has vanished. Lochbuie is one of only two remaining stone circles; a few standing stones appear here and there but nothing on the scale of Orkney or Lewis. There are echoes, though – traditions, folklore, names of places with vivid descriptions of a bygone era. Perhaps, like Orkney, Mull too was once governed by a triangular matrix of sacred places connected by a common purpose?

Sleep on it.

A whiff of haggis wafts under the bedroom door. Somewhere in the building, breakfast is being served. Who would ever imagine that offal mixed with suet and oatmeal, then boiled in a bag made from the animal's stomach was a culinary delight? I imagine it was developed to deter aliens from coming to Scotland and upsetting the sheep. *Mental note to develop this theory.*

Ever since reading an 18th century account about an initiatory cave on Mull – so long that people disappeared under Ben Mhor and reappeared on the opposite coast – I have wanted to find it for myself.[12] As improbable as it may seem, there is a precedent throughout Scotland for the use of caves during initiation rituals. One such ceremony was performed by the St. Thomas Lodge Freemasons of Arbroath, where initiates walked to Cove Haven on the Feast Day of John the Baptist, the main figure of veneration to the Knights Templar, whereupon new members were admitted following a restricted ceremony. Lit by flaming torches, candidates were marched two hundred feet into the belly of the cave to a spring at the very end.[13]

Below the highest cliffs of the west coast of Mull, MacKinnon's Cave was once connected with legends of initiates performing an ancient ritual while lying upon a massive flat stone called Fingal's Table, said to rest in a chamber far inside what sounds like a deep volcanic tube. Certainly its environs are protected by enough eerie superstition to keep the superficially curious away, and quite possibly designed with this intention in mind. As a back-up deterrent, the high tide flows inside the cave, leaving any hapless visitor to the mercy of threatening waves, enough to frighten the senseless and ensuring no one would ever advertise the location.

Reaching MacKinnon's Cave requires temperance, fortitude, and a slide down a cliff face on your bum (I'm sensing a pattern here) as well as a thorough understanding of tide charts. It is not a trek for the weak willed. And if this were indeed meant for initiation, then it fulfils the main criteria of the process: learning to conquer fear by overcoming a series of set obstacles. In Egypt, for example, candidates at the temple of Kom Ombu demonstrated this by swimming with live crocodiles.

Crocodiles are in short supply on Mull, but the beach has something equally treacherous: razor-sharp boulders covered in slick algae. After carefully maneuvering through these along the sliver of coast and past a waterfall one finally glimpses the entrance – a pointed cleft beneath a 400-foot vertical cliff. Should there be a rockfall you can console yourself in the knowledge you were buried by the second oldest rocks on Earth. The entrance into this divine womb couldn't be more dramatic. Impressed by the drama of it all, I took a few steps back to take in the scale of the setting. In doing so, I lost my concentration, slipped on the algae, and found myself lodged between sharp quartzite boulders, trapped upside down with a pain in my right arm and a warm, wet sensation dripping down my skin. I was bleeding. But none of this mattered because in less than one hour the tide would drown me.

Moments like these provide a stark choice between panic or the Mysteries teachings, and if this was the gods' way to test my fear, they were doing it convincingly. Show offs. I decided to take the path I've learned these past few decades – shove ice cubes down the vest of fear and relax. I mean, when you're faced with certain death what else could possibly go wrong!?

After a few minutes imitating a bat, I relaxed, let my body go limp, shifted my center of gravity, curved up like an eel around a boulder and slowly pried myself out of my predicament. News of my death would be premature this evening, my books would not be tripling in value. Regaining my focus on the aim of the adventure, I walked over to the sea, pulled out a length of seaweed and wrapped it around my bleeding arm. There's nothing quite like the feeling of saltwater on an open wound, with nothing but rocks to hear you scream.

KEEP CALM AND ENTER THE WOMB.

The small triangular cleft at the base of the cliff leads into a void resembling the dome of a cathedral. Between the dense rock and the sand piled inside by restless tides, every noise is muffled to the point where your heartbeat is the only sound. There is something unsettling about hearing nothing but your body – you are instantly reminded of the fragility and preciousness of this physical vessel. Wrapped in the absence of light, you are alone with whatever fear you still carry within. The space makes an ideal sensory deprivation chamber, and it is obvious why it would have been chosen above all other available caves. Back in ancient Egypt they built a massive structure to imitate this experience – the Kings Chamber of the Great Pyramid and its stone box, designed to illicit the very same response.

Looking out beyond the sliver of an entrance, the isle of Staffa sits on the horizon like a black dog, and beyond it the equinox sunset, another astronomical marker common to initiation chambers all around the world.[14] But where

1907 map referencing the cave.

was Fingal's Table, the preparatory stone once used by initiates who made the journey here, presumably by boat? About a hundred yards into the dark recess, the sand and ceiling inch closer together until further access is denied. In a matter of centuries, the sea has risen sufficiently to pile the sand deep into this tube, leaving nothing but personal observations from those who were still able to walk a considerable distance under the mountain, to reappear on the opposite coast of Mull. If the stories were true, all I needed to prove it was to locate the exit.

Back at the hotel I warned the manager there might be a wee bit of screaming. Not wanting to waste fine scotch, I dowsed cologne on my bruised arm and let the alcohol clean the wound. After posting a selfie of my arm (just to prove my research isn't done from a comfortable armchair) my attention returned to the day's adventure. If MacKinnon's Cave had indeed been used for initiation then the natural path for the candidate would have been to proceed until they emerged to face the equinox sunrise, as traditionally performed by ancient cultures throughout the world.[15]

To expect a natural cavity to run exactly east to west along the exact same degree of latitude, let alone beneath an entire island, would be an accomplishment in itself, and yet on maps dating back four centuries there is such an exit exactly due east of MacKinnon's Cave. Barely accessible at low tide nowadays, the mouth of the cave is sited below a vertical cliff and mirrors its counterpart in the west; a ruined passage mound still exists on an escarpment above. Its given name Uamh na Nighinn means Cave of the Young Maiden, an unusual choice given its isolated position away from any settlement, with no known local folklore pointing to a woman having lived or died there, so what might the name commemorate?

To anyone versed in the Mysteries, the name is highly symbolic. The path of initiation required the candidate to enter the womb of the Otherworld and cross a threshold where the sum of all knowledge resides. This wisdom was embodied in a divine bride to whom the successful candidate was symbolically wedded. Following the 'consummation' of this divine marriage the initiate exited the womb in time to gaze upon Venus rising just before the rising equinox Sun, the moment when the day and night, light and dark, are in perfect balance. The journey was physical as much as it was allegorical, with the cosmic marriage itself immortalized in myths such as Osiris and Isis, Tristan and Isolde, the Arthurian Grail quest, and so forth.[16]

The divine bride herself is associated with the Moon, and coincidentally, the distance between the two cave

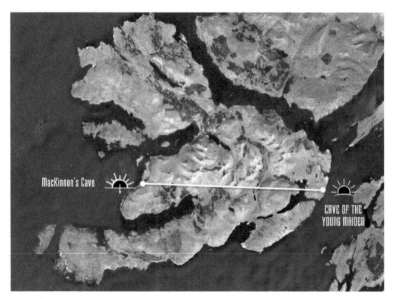

The initiate's path beneath Mull.

entrances is precisely 18.6 miles, the value in years
when the lunar cycle synchronizes with the solar, and
the masculine and feminine become a unified whole. To
pick out a cave under an island that conforms to this
numerical value is as astonishing an accomplishment as
it is impressive.

But there is a further layer of association here. The
Cave of the Young Maiden is located on a small, moon-
shaped beach called Port Donain. Officially it is named
for Donnán of Eigg, a 7th century Irish priest who brought
Christianity to the Inner Hebrides, an effort for which he
was beheaded. And yet Donnán never set foot on Mull.
Being an Irishman, perhaps his name is a corruption of
Danann, those gods of ancient Ireland mentioned earlier.

A third possibility is that Port Donain is a corruption
of *dun-ayq*, an Armenian phrase meaning 'house of dawn',
an apt description of the cave's functional solar alignment.
Incidentally, its variant *dun-ayr* means 'house-cave'.

With MacKinnon's Cave and the stone circle and
birthing chamber at Lochbuie I now had two locations tied
together by overlapping rituals, so perhaps there was a
third to complete a triangle, just as in Orkney. But where
might it be? The obvious place to start was Staffa, after
all it is the island seen from the mouth of MacKinnon's
Cave, and where this character called Fingal makes a
second appearance.

Five thousand years ago Staffa was separated from
Mull by a narrow river. Nowadays it is a bumpy twenty-
minute ride aboard an open fishing boat. The approach
to the island is otherworldly. Hexagonal basalt columns
rise vertically out of the sea creating a wall of black organ

pipes, punctuated by three caves. With the bottom of the ocean sometimes as little as twenty feet below the hull generating an agitated canvas of white, photographing this alien-looking world without bashing your skull on the deck is a challenge in itself, made all the more fun when the dark shadow of a ten-foot wave wraps the boat from behind. To watch the captain effortlessly glide his vessel in a dance with the sea is to witness a man who absolutely knows he is in control of fear.

The most prominent cave on Staffa is named after Fingal, or to be precise, Finn mac Cumhaill, the mythological Gaelic hunter-warrior in the same vein as Jason the Argonaut, or Osiris. This intrepid individual retrieves a treasure, accidentally eats the salmon of knowledge, encounters his lady while hunting, watches her transformed into a deer by a Druidhe, and spends the rest of his life looking for this divine bride. Then, after passing three strenuous tests, he is admitted to the court of the king of Ireland at Tara, whereupon he becomes a great leader. Another happy ending.

Fionnghall is not so much a name as a title: 'white stranger', obviously a person who came from elsewhere,

Staffa. On a calm day.

with a physiognomy sufficiently different for local people to write it into legend. He was also very tall, often portrayed as a benevolent giant who tosses parts of Ireland as stepping stones to Scotland, a literary mechanism allegorically describing how the history of both lands is umbilically connected by the knowledge of the gods. We are dealing here with a supernatural man of kingly, possibly divine descent, who is unusually tall, white-skinned and comes from a faraway place. To round off his already impressive resumé, Fionnghall is guardian of the passage into Annwn, the Gaelic Otherworld, and, like others of his kind, he is accompanied in this task by two supernatural black hounds. And just like Osiris, he too is associated with Orion.

This forensic mythological information builds a picture of the kind of people who might have been responsible for the Western Isles' sacred practices, its megalithic culture, or both.

Once on Staffa, the tide recedes and one is able to walk the basalt columns by the edge of the sea without being wary of incoming waves. It feels like walking along a billion-year old beehive. The three caves along the southern basalt wall – two large, one small – brought to mind the stone circles on Orkney and their mirroring of the belt stars of Orion, so on a hunch I located the caves on a topographic map to see whether the same relationship was taking place here, especially given Fionnghall's connection with Orion. Figuratively standing in front of the caves of Staffa to face the southern horizon, a marvelous sight presented itself on the spring equinox in 3000 BC, when the three stars forming the Belt of Orion rose out of the sea for the first time at this location.

It seems the legend of Fionnghall – whether he was a real person, a mythological figure, or a combination of both – provides information as to when this island may have first been consecrated and used as a landscape temple. In the context of Orkney and Lewis, the dates are getting younger, like an arc descending from the north, along the Western Isles, inching ever closer to Ireland.

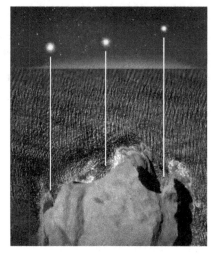

Relationship of caves to Orion.

But something was missing. Staffa itself does not fit an obvious geodetic pattern with the other two locations on Mull. My search for the third site, potentially forming a perfect triangle with Lochbuie and MacKinnon's Cave, was incomplete. Taking the distance between these two locations, 11.8 miles, the same distance taken in the opposite direction places a mark right in the middle of an island of profound spiritual significance: Iona.

The timetable for the ferry crossing from Mull to Iona reads SHIP DEPARTS 10:05, SHIP ARRIVES 10:10. It is never late, apparently. Even during a gale, when my ferry approached the quay sideways, the inconvenience of adverse weather is minimal, a testament to old-fashioned skill. Having arrived almost lengthways at Iona, I made my way to a quiet place I know where one can partake of a rare whisky that is both unspellable and unpronounceable, and waited for the billowing wind to run out of breath.

Over the decades I've witnessed the eroding of Iona's ancient history from visitor information boards, brochures and books, forcing those with a hunger for truth to dig a little deeper. I remember a time when a woman minister led a most enchanting Celtic Christian mass in the abbey. It began: "We honor the elements of earth, air, fire, water and the central force that binds them in balance." When the moment came for the sermon, anyone in the congregation with something appropriate to share was offered the pulpit – on this occasion it was the gardener, who read from an article describing how people function best when working in harmony with rather than in opposition to nature. It nearly made me join the Church, and for several hours I actually meant it. Sadly this utopia has since been replaced. What was once a subtle Christian presence on the island is now overt, with more and more pilgrims arriving at the pier carrying a weight on their shoulders, often in the shape of an imaginary wooden cross.

Still, there is every reason to be optimistic on this small rocky outcrop in the middle of the ocean because some unseen force has been luring people here since at least 3500 BC, to the point where Iona became the burial place of choice for no less than eight Danish and Norwegian sea kings, forty Hebridean kings and queens, the Scottish Alba kings and queens, along with one British prime minister, an unknown king of France and, last but not least, Macbeth.

Even the megalith builders made the vexing sea journey here. A dolmen with seven-foot tall stones once stood somewhere on the west side of the island. As did a black meteoric stone, similar to the Kaaba in Mecca, which was given a place of honor in the abbey and became the focus of pilgrimage until it vanished in 1830 under suspicious circumstances. The site of the abbey was originally occupied by a circle of 360 stones, still standing in 1560 when the Protestant Synod of Argyle ordered such "monuments of idolatrie be cast into the sea" – by hypocrites who re-carved at least twelve of them with Christian symbols of idolatry.[17]

Coincidentally the Kaaba in Mecca originally contained 360 idols and was dedicated to a deity named Hubal,[18] whose origin is said to be Mesopotamia.[19]

That's quite a long history for a rock three miles by one and you'll come across little of it during your peregrination. The Church deftly whitewashed other juicy stuff, such as Iona's most ancient known Gaelic name Inish Druinidh, 'island of the sorcerers, magicians, wise people'. The Celtic variant, *druidh,* means 'to enclose within a circle', a title used in the context of an individual who is admitted into the Mysteries of an inner religious group. Its proto-Indo-European root *dru* means 'firm, steadfast', from which derive the words 'truth' and 'tree'.[20] Furthermore, *druis* derives from *truwis,* meaning 'a doctor of faith', along with its Germanic variant *trowis,* 'a revealer of truth'. With so many overlaps in dialect and structure between Celtic, Gaelic and Phoenician languages,[21]

Crosses carved from original menhirs.

it is not surprising to see the same word echoed in the Hebrew *Deerussim*, meaning 'contemplators'.

The language and place names of the Western Isles bear many surprising similarities to those of the Levant.[22] For example, the Palestinian religious site Cana is shared with the Scottish isle of Canna, where a broken slab of yellow sandstone in its churchyard is carved with unknown symbols and the image of a camel, the sole instance of such an animal in Scottish religious

iconography.[23] It implies the movement of people to this
region from the Mediterranean, one of whom was a son of
Joseph of Arimathea who married a daughter of a king of
the Western Isles.[24] With these fragments we are offered a
picture of an island of Druidhe, of magicians, wise people,
seekers of truth, and contemplators of a spiritual path.

Another religious group who made its way from the
Levant to establish a home in Iona was the Culdee – who
we encountered earlier as the Khaldi of Armenia. Their
arrival in 37 AD [25] is frowned upon or simply ignored by
the usual suspects, and yet a look at the oldest maps of
Iona defines an area adjacent to the present abbey, Cladh
an Diseart, as a hermitage belonging to the Culdee. The
early ecclesiastical foundations of Ireland and Scotland
are based on this concept of *Disart* or *Desart,* a relic of the
Egyptian hermetic tradition whereby practitioners sought
solitary quests in a deserted environment. Or to put it in
Christian terminology, a wilderness, much like the one
Jesus retired to for forty days that led him to confront his
inner demons and conquer his animal nature, his fear. I
wonder how many Christian pilgrims disembarking on
Iona are consciously aware that it is this ancient initiatory
practice that most likely drew them here?

The Culdee preserved traditions already established
by the Druidhe, and by the 6th century the hermits were
still living in the Disaert. The ruins of a small oratory
are still there today. Yet even this wilderness was
far too urban for some monks. Those desiring a more
deserted wilderness retired to a beehive chamber marked
Cobhanculdich on a map from 1860, located on the south-
western slope of the hill behind the abbey.

The tolerant worldview of the Culdee was far removed
from that of St. Columba and the other twelve misogynists
who invaded Iona in 563 AD, wishing to "represent the
pinnacle of Christian virtues as an example for others to

emulate." [26] This from a leader who'd earlier instigated a rebellion in Ireland that led to the death of 3000 people and his subsequent expulsion from the country.[27] The Druidhe didn't care much for Columba either, they are said to have conjured the weather against him after he tried to kick them off the island that had been their home for so long it even bore their name. But Columba persevered and built his monastery adjacent to the Culdee chapel, appropriating the ruins of an earlier 4th century building.

When Vikings raiders visited Iona from time to time, whilst they looted the Columban monastery and massacred its monks, they surprisingly left the Culdee and their chapel alone. The Vikings' respect for the Culdee, and their abhorrence of Columba and what his people represented, speaks volumes about the politics of the period and how the story has been politically skewed. Columba singlehandedly whitewashed Iona's pre-history before turning his sights on the nearby Nunnery and expelling all women from Iona. He obviously also upset the spirit of the land because by the 9th century, despite his influence throughout Scotland and northeast England, his successors had led the monastic community into decay.

What little remained was raised from the dead at the end of the 11th century by an order of monks from Cluny, with assistance from the Cistercian Order and its head Bernard de Clairvaux, who had begun his ministerial duties at Cluny before emerging as head of the Cistercians, and later, the central figure behind the Knights Templar.[28] Given a

Iona Abbey in 1833

new lease on life, Iona reclaimed its spiritual mojo during the 12th century. The Benedictine monks made improvements to the abbey, the Culdee continued their ruminations in the desert, and Reginald, son of Somerled, Lord

A dragon marks a telluric current inside the abbey.

of the Isles, together with his sister Bethóc built a Nunnery on the site of the earlier building, allowing the black nuns to return from Eilean nam Ban and resume work on the island.[29]

It always puzzled me why the Vikings left one specific chapel unmolested during their rampages. The Odhràn chapel was named after a companion of Columba who'd taken it upon himself to restore the building formerly used by the displaced Culdee, and apparently, where they practiced an unspecified secret ritual. Just like Cainnech's chapel and its vortex in Lochbuie, there is a special quality inside this room, in fact, it feels much more holy than the adjacent abbey. Most visitors overlook this place in favor of the grander building beyond, but the few who stay notice a special energy here and are loathe to leave. Strangely enough there is a legend that backs up these impressions, and it survives thanks to Odhràn.

Odhràn came across a legend that the walls of the chapel came down as fast as they went up as though by evil magic. Only when a person was buried alive would the stones stay put. Being the devout Catholic, Odhràn thought little of this pagan mumbo jumbo, but to his credit he volunteered to be buried alive to prove the point. Three days later the earth was removed, Odhràn raised himself, and much to everyone's bewilderment, the monk declared that "all that had been preached about hell is a

Odhran's Chapel.

joke!" Odhràn, it seems, had had himself an out-of-body experience, traveled to the Otherworld, and returned to tell the tale of how the universe really is rather than how it is portrayed by religion. As with all places used for this initiatory exercise, the chapel is sited on a hotspot of geomagnetic energy capable of facilitating such a journey. The concept of walls going down and up is an allegorical description of the change in perception experienced during the ritual – the dematerialization of the physical world and with it the temporary departure of the soul and its eventual return to the living body. Eastern mystics called it Tayi. In the west we came to know it as The Way via the Essenes, who, like the Druidhe, referred to themselves as 'Sons of Light'.[30] The earliest known practitioner of this initiation was a god-man of the Indus Valley from c.6500 BC called Mithras. I go into precise detail about this spiritual technology in my earlier book *The Lost Art of Resurrection.*

The former Culdee chapel has one more surprise up its sleeve, and it concerns the denial by academia of the Culdee's presence on Iona in 37 AD. The chapel is aligned to the rising of Venus before sunrise on the spring equinox on this exact date. It is the same cosmic mark commemorated at Moy Castle and the Cave of the Young Maiden, and for that matter in temples and chambers from Britain to Bolivia used for the final and most secret part of the initiatory process, the moment when the candidate faces the morning star and is declared "risen from the dead."[31] Originating in the Orient and traveling west to the Near East, the ritual would have been well known to practitioners of the Mysteries, such as the Culdee.

How does all this relate to our Neolithic adventure and the third point of the elusive triangle? Aside from references to earlier megalithic structures, it doesn't. The Culdee chapel is about a mile off the mark, and for the hypothesis to be correct a more precise monument would be required.

The ferry timetable read LAST FERRY 6:15. Five minutes later I was back on Mull.

What good is a bed and breakfast without an *en suite* beach and a standing stone? The early evening light draped sand, crags and sea in a calm patina of platinum blue, while the lethargic shore was perforated by the head of seal examining the guy on the beach studying an old map.

The highest point on the southern side of Iona used to be called Hill of the Druids, where the white-robed priests partook in midsummer celebrations. Perhaps the third point of the triangle had been this obvious all along. But no, the marker was still off by half a mile. Among my reading material was a personal account by Thomas Pennant, a traveler and writer who visited Iona in 1772 and came across a cairn and a circle of stones.[32] A map of the period validates Pennant's observation, listing the site as Cnoc an Aingeal, literally 'Hill of Angels'. This was the second time I'd come across angels in connection with megalithic sites, the other being the area between lochs Stenness and Harray on Orkney, known in antiquity as the Bay of Angels for reasons that remain lost in the mist of cultural amnesia.

On the other hand, the origin of 'angel' might fill in the blanks. In the original Greek translation of the Bible the word *aggelos* means 'messengers', and the term referred not to ethereal beings but to real people called Watchers – ambassadors for another, yet more elevated group.[33] Both originated in the general area of the Armenian Highlands, the region that spawned a civilization which progressed the legacy of humanity thousands of years ahead of natural evolution: Sumeria.[34] The original scribe of this story, Enmed Ur-anu (later transliterated as Enoch) describes these light-skinned people wearing white linen garments[35] who inscribed "the

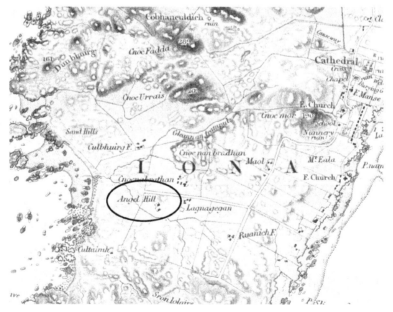

Hill of the Angels on an 1860 map of Iona.

signs of heaven" on stones, strongly implying that the Watchers were intimately knowledgeable of the motions of the stars and sky, a knowledge referred to as "the Science of the Watchers."[36] In other words, these 'angels' were astronomers who immortalized their knowledge in stone. And the one constellation with which they were associated was Orion.

To reflect their status as learned individuals they were nicknamed Shining Ones, immediately conjuring the folklore at Callanish and how a Shining One walked the avenue of stones during midsummer venerations.

Suddenly, things began falling into place regarding the origin of the mysterious builders of temples on the Scottish islands.

While the cairn and the stones are now long gone, the Hill of Angels still exists as an unassuming mound called Sithean Mòr, 'hill of the Fairy People'. Standing on its summit you can still make out the telltale teardrop shape common to man-made passage mounds, with a flattened, dimpled face in the north, presumably the entrance into the chamber. That said, since the mound has yet to be excavated we are none the wiser as to whether such a

The teardrop outline of the Hill of Angels.

chamber exists, but, given its general axis, it is possible to take a bead to the horizon and see what it might have been looking at and when. With the general direction of the dimple at 35° NE, the reference is to the Major Lunar Standstill, with the mound's axis referencing the setting Moon. If you face the opposite direction – since we do not know on which side the entrance might be – you get the most revealing alignment of all: Orion and Sirius rising before the winter solstice in 3600 BC.

We appear to be looking at a continuation of practice and intent on Iona that began two thousand years earlier on Orkney. If all this is correct, then the Hill of Angels must once have been an artificial site now devoid of stones. Could this be the third point of the triangle?

Take a line from MacKinnon's Cave to Lochbuie stone circle, 11.8 miles, and from the cave to the Hill of Angels, 11.8 miles. A perfect isosceles triangle.

Given the extreme terrain over which this alignment was created, the ancient surveyors were nothing short of magicians – tall "strangers from afar" who wore the white tunics symbolic of fairness and truth. And prior to their accomplishments in Scotland they may have left their fingerprint further to the south, in the Mediterranean.

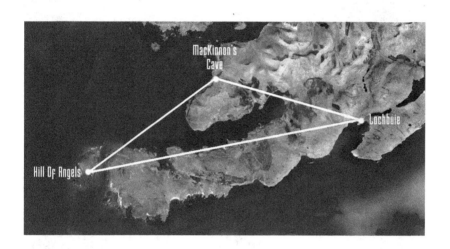

*One of the many unusual inhabitants
of Sardinia.*

8

LAND OF THE BRIDE
OF THE SUN

ven the locals apologized for the absurd amount of rain. "Seen nothing like it in three hundred years." "The weather is never like this, even in winter. It's not winter." And it would have been acceptable had I been in Britain, except I was checking into my hotel in Cagliari, capital of typically sunny Sardinia.

When I was twelve my history teacher taught me that in order to understand a culture or a tradition one must take a distant view, be it epochal or geographical. Little did I know just how accurate this advice would prove to be in solving this Scottish riddle, which is why I found myself traveling to one of the most geologically ancient lands in Europe, inhabited since the Upper Paleolithic, home to a civilization that left nothing by way of writing. Many words, dialects, names of mountains and rivers on this vast island have no basis in Greek, Latin, Punic or Semitic languages, but instead show analogies with Basque and North Libyan, and dialects from along the Danube River, indicating remnants of a language left behind by a former, now forgotten civilization.[1]

Among all the lands I've explored, Sardinia ranks as one of the strangest. For starters, no one can agree on the origin of its name or inhabitants. Letters found in Akhenaten's city, Akhetaten, refer to the island's inhabitants as Srdn-w, seafarers and raiders who may have originated in Asia Minor and moved to Sardinia after the collapse of Minoan supremacy, but this was a comparatively recent event.[2]

Then there's DNA. Due to their isolation, Sardinians carry a unique genetic heritage, the DNA of their ancestors from 10,000 BC survives in the modern population. An analysis of the mitochondrial DNA of 3,500 inhabitants, representing all the provinces on the island, was compared with that extracted from twenty-one prehistoric ancestors found in archaeological sites between 4000-2000 BC. The data was then compared with 50,000 modern and 500 ancient genomes related to the entire world population. The results show Sardinians maintain 78.4 percent of genetic heritage linked to ethnic groups dating to the early Neolithic, a record in Europe.[3]

Even more of a mystery is Sardinia's long tradition of unusual sacred places, rock-cut chambers, passage mounds, standing stones, and their associations to fairies or witches or giants. As always, they are officially herded into the same convenient box: tombs.

Sardinian faeries are called *janas*. They appear as small, beautiful winged women who generate a blinding light, dress in red and wear hats embroidered with silver thread. According to tradition, each newborn baby is assigned a protective *jana* who watches over the soul. And yet *jana* is not a local word, it originates with the Mesopotamian *jina*, whose root *j-n-n* means 'hidden'. In time it developed into *jannah*, the Islamic concept of paradise, along with its derivative *janela*, which originally meant 'a window into another country'. In Indian religious practices, particularly in the Jain culture, those who gain mastery over the physical world and achieve a state of godliness are to this day awarded the title *Jina*. These terms subsequently migrated to Europe as the Latin *genius,* 'a tutelary spirit attendant on a person', a personal guardian angel, and by the 17th century it transmuted further into *genie*.

Thus faery sites in Sardinia, rather than being the final domicile of dead people, are in fact portals of subtle energy that either elevate an individual into a paradisal state – another country indeed – or behave as points of transmutation between terrestrial and etheric locations. Certainly they were never originally intended for burial, and the older generation in villages throughout Sardinia knows this. Nor were the *domus de gianas*, 'tombs of the witches', the name given to structures incorporating two or more chambers. Menhirs and other standing stones are often found in their vicinity, some bearing breasts carved in relief, a subtle hint that rites of fertility rather than death once took place here.

To further our understanding of who the Neolithic magicians might have been, we add *tomba di giganti*, literally 'giant's graves', except no giants have ever been found inside these unusual passage mounds, at least according to official figures. Edmund Bouchier, like most explorers, mentions the giants' graves scattered throughout the island yet makes no attempt to explain why such a description might have been given,[4] and ever since, an air of mystery has hung over Sardinia.

By the time ancient Greeks arrived on the scene, only myths remained of islanders being the rudimentary progeny of earlier god-men, although Sardinians do have the highest concentration of dolichocephalic skulls (long heads) in Europe.[5] The historian Diodorus Siculus compiled a treasure trove of information on the persistent rumors that the island was once associated with the flood era god-man Heracles. The gist of the legend is this: after Heracles performed his twelve labors, the gods persuaded him to create a colony in Sardinia and make his sons its leaders, which he did, along with his charioteer, the Argonaut Iolaus, for which he was finally allowed to join the company of the gods.

Heracles was half human, half divine, borne of the mating of a god with a human woman, the Mediterranean equivalent of the Mesopotamian flood hero Gilgamesh, who was himself part human, part Apkallu (sage). Since one of Heracles' labors was to catch the Cretan Bull, ostensibly he is also the human embodiment of Orion the Hunter chasing Taurus the Bull. Like his Egyptian *doppëlganger* Osiris, Heracles was associated with fertility and the Otherworld, as is Orion. Coinci-

Figurine depicting an ancient Sardinian.

dentally, Gilgamesh was associated with the same con-stellation, which is listed in Babylonian star catalogues as Sipa.Zi.An.Na, 'True Shepherd of Ana/Anu'. The point to bear in mind here is that the root of Orion is *Oarion*, a Greek transliteration of the Mesopotamian sage Ur-anu, who we encountered earlier. Depending on the source language his name translates as 'light of the sky' or 'Red Man of Anu' and is formally linked with a group of people mentioned fleetingly in previous chapters, the Tuadhe d'Anu.

All this mythology may come across as light entertainment, yet it is important to understand that myth is a theatrical mechanism used to encode valuable historical information in a manner that assists the memorializing of important events. Although the language and symbolism employed may sometimes be obtuse to our ears, the events and people portrayed in the stories are faithfully recorded for posterity. For one thing, the legend of Heracles is encoded with astronomical data.

When myths and legends are experienced collectively by native people and their ancestors, they become the backbone of folkloric memory. To brush aside such rich information is a detriment to our understanding of the past. My first visit to Sardinia was in the company of researcher and television presenter Regina Meredith, and investigative journalist Paola Harris. One of the highlights of this collaboration was an introduction to Luigi Muscas, resident of the village of Pauli Arbarei, who has documented the testimonies of his family and village elders, as well as his own lifetime of experiences among Sardinia's rich Neolithic landscape. Not only do they echo the myths and traditions encountered by ancient travelers, they provide first-hand accounts of what exactly has been taking place on their island.

Many people in the central highlands recall direct

encounters with what they describe as "stars falling from the sky," one of these being Luigi's grandmother. "She was the first to tell me stories about the stars. She told me that the stars used to come down from the sky, brightening, and they stopped just above the most beautiful persons or animals. She'd been watching them since she was a child... the stars of the giants... like my great-great-grandfather, who was 7.4 feet tall, who saw a globe falling from the sky. It was white, light blue and red; it was emanating warmth and making a subtle rustle."[6]

Luigi's uncle, Geraldo, recalls the same experience: "After a few minutes a star lit up and came down to us; I was amazed and enchanted. Soon after, another one, even bigger, landed next to us. I was so emotional I could do nothing other than kneel and make the sign of the cross. Since then, I sit outside every day and admire the stars and spend at least an hour with them."[7]

After centuries of collective interactions with these orbs it was calculated they occur in a roughly triangular area around Pauli Arbarei.[8]

There were also experiences of a more physical nature. Rummaging in his family's farmlands, Luigi would come across entire skeletons of people up to fifteen feet tall, which his friends often came over to play with. "It was the 18th of February, 1972. I was, as usual, herding the sheep after school when a thunderstorm forced me to find shelter in a cave. There I found a huge skeleton, the dimensions of which, I realized, were far above the norm. To give you an idea, the head was as big as a 26-inch television, but with a rounded shape. The upper limbs were as long as I was, about 4 feet. What caught my attention even more was the fact that the body seemed to be mummified. It still had all its skin and below that you could see the ligaments. The skin had a color like cappuccino. [My grandfather] explained to me that *"cuss'omi mannu"* [this big man] was nothing but one of the ancestors of our folk that lived in the age of the lost city... This was a folk of sailors and conquerors that belonged to a highly evolved culture. He showed me the remains of the walls of the city in a place we call Sa Contissa... He continued with the story, talking about the temples and showing me a few of them – which were well preserved – close to the *nuraghe* that surrounded the city. I asked him where these folks came from and he replied that they came from the sky and that they used to venerate the moon and the stars through sacred rituals and that the place where I found the skeleton was used for this religious purpose... The new folks started to build temples, *nuraghe* and pyramids, not just in Sardinia but also in Corsica, which, at the time, was linked to Sardinia [around 11,000 years ago]. According to the legend, they used to have a fleet of 1,200 ships they used to travel around the world, spreading their wisdom and culture...

Those extraordinary people knew astronomy, mathematics, and medicine."[9]

Another resident, Gesualdo Pilloni, recalls the discovery of giants even by the previous generation: "In 1944 my father leased some lands where there was a tomb of giants three times larger than the one found in Siddi. But, in those lands there was not only one grave, but, under an eight inch-thick slab, many remains of the ancient city as well as the remains of columns, temples, floors... It seems that 3,000 skulls of giant humans have been found inside the tomb. All destroyed by bulldozers and modern plows. As long as farmers used the ancient methods, graves and other riches remained intact and protected."[10] Ten years later, excavators at Porto Torres uncovered two, eight-foot tall intact skeletons estimated to be 4000 years old, buried with weapons, furnishings and vases. The report made Reuters and was subsequently published around the world. [11]

Two things struck me after listening to accounts such as these (and there are a lot of them): first, this civilization had a long track record of seafaring, astronomy and mathematics, the three central requirements needed by the "strangers from afar" to create the megalithic culture in the isles of Scotland. This ticked a few boxes. And second, of all the skeletons found in graves in fields, not one came from the elaborate passage mounds, the *tomba di giganti*. Some were unearthed by accident during the island's road extension program, as Luigi recalls: "During the spring of 1975, the discovery of a new *giganti* was announced. During that time, work was being done on the road from Siddi and Lunamatrona to the border of Pauli Arbarei, and that day there were many men at work. I went there by bike with the other two friends to see the giant. The workers didn't let us get closer, so we stopped 30 meters away upon a little hill. Regardless of a large number of people surrounding the grave from which the skeleton was taken, we could see him perfectly from our position and his size was truly huge. Compared to him, the people around him looked like children.... In 1977 I was with some friends on the road that goes from Pauli Arbarei to Las Plassas, close to the area of Sa Contissa, where they were again carrying out road work. We found the skeletons of two giants inside of a grave. We supposed by their position that they were embracing each other. The next morning, when we went there to check, the skeletons where gone... Every time a skeleton was found, the priest of our village said to break it in pieces or to burn it because that skeleton was to be considered a demon... In every case, all the findings had to disappear."[12]

According to additional testimony by another eyewitness, Benvenuto Cau, one of these skeletons "was more than 9 feet, more or less the size of a Fiat Uno."[13]

Virgilio Saiu not only heard about giants, in his time he saw more than his fair share: "I saw the first two skeletons with my father in Albagiara, the land in which I was born and raised, while we were building a wall. I was 17 and I remember that, while we were laying the foundation, we found two very large stone slabs. We lifted one with an iron lever and discovered a tomb with a huge skeleton, about 12 feet long. Immediately we went to the Podesta's home and the skeletons were taken away. Years later, in Pauli Arbarei, my wife's country, I and other workers were laying the foundations of a house for Francesco Lai, situated behind the church of St. Augustine. We found a huge tomb. It was 1950. There was also a giant buried there. The tomb is larger than 12 feet and inside one section we found a skeleton still wearing clothes... He still had all his teeth — the dimensions were about the same as the finger of an adult man; and very large nostrils, about like the fist of an adult hand. We measured the fingers. They were eight inches long. It

struck me that the body was mummified. He still had all his joints, ligaments, skin. What happened to the skeleton? We left him there, buried under the foundations of the house, covered by stone and cement. Nobody understood the importance of the discovery...The slabs covered 20 tombs of giants of about 9 and 12 feet tall. I remember the landowner told us to leave the skeletons where they were without disclosing the discovery, otherwise they would have stopped the work on the vineyard."[14]

Sometimes the bones were of extreme age and crumbled easily. Others were better preserved and Luigi collected a fair number. But as word spread of the discoveries, many were appropriated by the authorities, dumped in heaps and covered with soil to be forgotten. Harassment from archaeologists or priests was said to be commonplace, but in the countryside, people possess the gift of long memory, and the stories are handed from generation to generation lest they be buried too. According to the testimony by Giuseppe Pulisci, who was an archaeologist: "In 1981 I was part of the group that performed archaeological excavation at the nuragic village of St. Anastasia. During the work we carried off, if I remember correctly, thirteen skeletons of giants measuring between 8 to 11 feet long. Along with the skeletons there were so many everyday objects: pottery of various types, coins, bronzes; moreover, every skeleton was still wearing gold rings, bracelets, and various jewelry. We put them inside the Church of St. Anastasia, but when we entered the church the next day, we noticed that they were gone. This happened every time we found a skeleton. Surely, they were taken somewhere else after the end of our working hours. I went to the city to ask that those skeletons be preserved and exhibited in Sardara, as a testimony to one of our ancient cultures, but they told me to "mind my own business" if I wanted to continue to work at those jobs."[15]

Antonello Garau further illustrates the palpable frustration among local inhabitants: "In 1972, during an outing to look for snails in the area Corte Baccasa, just above the pyramid on the land of Tzia Licca, I saw a scene unfold just like an action movie. At about 120 feet from me, where there is a tomb of the giants, seven people arrived who I did not know and suddenly a helicopter landed. I sat down to watch the scene. I saw a giant skeleton, which was loaded on to the helicopter and after that, they opened another tomb, next to the first one. From there they pulled out a skeleton that joined the other one on the helicopter. Then they went away quickly."[16]

There is a unique sense of pride among older Sardinians that they are descended from an elevated culture, genetically and culturally, even if few today physically resemble their remote ancestors. But if no *giganti* were buried in the *tomba di giganti*, the name given to the structures must come from a folk memory of people of very tall stature becoming synonymous with the monuments they created.

Since one of the ancient migrants to Sardinia are known to have originated from North Africa, it is interesting that the Tuareg have similar megalithic mounds and standing stones attributed to Izabbaren, an ancient race of giants who preceded them. The name derives from *jabbar*, the Arabic for 'giant'. The women still consult these ancient sacred places, being careful to avoid wearing objects or iron or steel, even a needle, which may interfere with the communication process. They lie beside the mound until the attendant *zabbar* appears to them in the form of a giant with large eyes. The women make a notable distinction between these as places of consultation with the spirit world compared to places of physical burial.[17]

Unlike traditional burial places, the *tomba di giganti*,

or passage mounds of Sardinia are designed as though they are collecting something and looking out to the horizon. Generally speaking, they consist of a long and very narrow box made from a combination of horizontal and vertical slabs of stone, then covered with earth to give them a pleasant curving contour, broad at the front and tapering towards the rear – much like the Hill of Angels on Iona.

What makes them truly unique is the forecourt, where a path of short standing stones has been set like a crescent Moon or a pair of horns. A thin *stela* marks the entrance, anywhere up to 17 feet tall and carved with three concave sections, the lowest perforated by a hole barely large enough to accommodate a very small pig. Save for the forecourt *stela* we may as well be describing the horned passage mounds of Orkney, because that is exactly what they resemble. We are asked to believe that much time and effort was employed to make an elegant stone chamber to preserve the integrity of an important individual yet some fool carved a large hole for vermin to scavenge the corpse and undermine the entire enterprise. Thinking of these monuments as tombs, therefore, is counter-productive, if not counter-intuitive.

From inside the chamber, however, the hole offers a fabulous view on the edge of high ground to a notch on the horizon or a designated expanse of sky, as though the

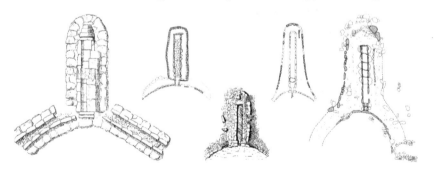

Tomba di giganti.

Tomba di giganti, Iloi.
Chambers of oldest sites are
superior in quality, with perfectly
fitted large stone blocks.

chamber and its curved forecourt are engaged in attracting an object under observation, the light of the Sun, the Moon, perhaps an alignment to a constellation or star,[18] even the gathering of telluric current, which all such sites across the world share in common.[19] None of the above are of any use to a decaying corpse.

But to the living it's another matter, especially those who understood the relationship between forces that bind the Earth and the cosmos, who knew that the alignment to specific objects brought beneficial forces to bear on the land and those who relied on it for survival and spiritual attuning. And local folklore tells us much about the way people interacted

Coddu Vecchiu.

with these structures and what they might have expected from them. If we can accept that the so-called 'tombs'

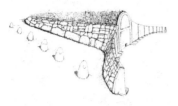

are associated with tall beings of the physical and non-physical variety, returning to the belief that Sardinians are the progeny of a race of giants leads us to a basic assumption that the passage mounds have been handed down from a remote era. The question is, how old might they be?

Traditions circulating throughout the island associate the *giganti* with Orion, so let's put this to the test.[20] Using the mound Su Monte'e S'Abe as a random example, it aligns to the rising of Orion and Sirius on the winter solstice in 4000 BC, what turned out to be one of the youngest archaeoastronomical dates for Sardinia. A second mound, Sa Doand Orrida marks the Major Lunar Standstill, as well as Orion on the winter solstice in 5200 BC. After these two, things got progressively older.

My favorite, the horned *tomba di giganti* at Iloi, may have lost all its soil cover but not its sense of drama, perched as it is at the very edge of a steep mesa where a careless

Entrance stela.
S'Ena 'e Thomes.

selfie will have you making contact with an unyielding surface 500 feet below. The hole in its entrance *stela* offers an exceptional view of a large lake and a mountainous horizon above which Orion reached its mid-heaven position on the winter solstice in 7200 BC. The same date reference occurs at the passage mound in Osono.

Imbertighe is yet another example. Its horned forecourt

Tomba di giganti, Osono.
Now minus its soil cover.

and phallic fifteen-foot tall entrance *stela* faces the equinox sunrise in 8500 BC, while Li Loighi memorializes the winter solstice on the same date.

With so many mounds still to be examined, the present assessment reveals a megalithic culture in Sardinia preceding that of Orkney and Lewis, yet sharing the same traits in construction style, astronomical alignment, tradition and mythology. Additionally, the extreme date of 8500 BC brings Sardinia in line with archaeological evidence and culturally shared mythology of an era when humanity suddenly discovered civilization at hotspots around the world – the Near East and the Nile Valley in particular. What all these events share in common is an interaction between hunter gatherers and tall gods displaced by a global flood who arrive from their sunken lands with the aim of assisting humans in restarting civilization.[21]

The other thing all these gods and sages shared in common? They were master seafarers and astronomers, all associated with Orion. One by one the congruencies between Sardinia and Scotland are reducing the gap

Li Loighi.

between hearsay and fact. Perhaps the other monuments ancient Sardinians left behind can narrow it further.

One inescapable fact dominates this island: it is covered with over 6500 stone towers. Historians place them anywhere between 3500-1500 BC yet little carbon dating has been performed to validate this range. Instead, just as in nearby Malta, the sites have been arbitrarily allocated a time-frame that best fits the academic model, one that relies on pottery shards or animal bones buried in accumulated layers of dirt. Realistically, the people who built such impressive monuments would hardly have allowed soil, broken pottery and decomposing animal parts to be strewn inside the buildings, thus the dating can only inform us of a period long after the sites had fallen into decline, filled with detritus, and were reoccupied. Thus, if the lowest habitation layer dates to 3500 BC, the sites must be considerably older.

During my time traveling through Sardinia, browsing its bookstores and libraries and reading up on history written by people who were born, lived and died there, one glaring problem soon presented itself: the towers, like its culture, are called *nuraghe*, yet no book, plaque or person can explain the origin or meaning of this word that has come to define an entire culture. How could this be possible? Standard academic explanations are wanting, at best: *nuraghe* derives from Nura, an early name given to Minorca, a small Spanish island on the opposite side of the Mediterranean; or that it originates from the Phoenician word *nur* (fire),[22] allegedly because beacons were lit atop the towers to warn of incoming troublemakers. Having visited a fair number of them, I find this opinion unsustainable at best. Examples such as Nuraghe Is Paras feature a single beehive chamber whose ceiling tapers to an open hole, as though designed to observe passing stars. Lighting a bonfire would shower

red-hot embers on the occupants below, and since there
are no traces of soot or creosote on the internal walls, no
one was lighting fires from within either.

Where *nuraghe* are separated by a mere 500 yards,
a simple wave of a flag would have sufficed as a means
of communication, and far more subtle; where they stand
alone in valleys, no one else would be around to see the
smoke from a beacon. You'd only be setting fire to your
own building. Unsatisfied I decided to widen my gaze.

Nuraghe Ponte.

The highest concentration of *nuraghe* is throughout the high plains and mountainous regions of the island. They often stand alone atop an artificial mound resembling a pregnant belly, founded on megalithic stonework using no mortar, and often made from interlocked blocks of basalt, not exactly the easiest building material to work with. Others are made from blocks of granite, lava, or tufa, as well as an unusual type of coarse limestone, a far softer material to cut and shape. Some blocks used for architraves measure as much as 12 feet in length and depth,[23] but millennia of earthquakes and warfare necessitated periodic rebuilding using progressively smaller, more practical masonry. The tallest *nuraghe* reach 90 feet, tapering as they rise, and the best preserved feature a central beehive chamber as much as twenty-five feet high, with further chambers placed atop in diminishing size and proportion to the external inclination. Two to four niches, each the size of a small bookshelf, are set into the walls, generally at ground level. Access to the upper chambers is via a spiral corridor set inside the main wall, with connecting corridors and corbel arches echoing Mycenaean and eastern Mediterranean architectural traditions.[24] Despite their simplicity the *nuraghe* are wonderfully strong, and the peculiar direction and smallness of entrance, the narrow winding passages, domed chambers, small aperture for the admission of light, all seem to point to a restricted or astronomical function.

Asking for an opinion of the nature of the *nuraghe* is like asking for a definitive explanation of a black hole: tombs of antediluvian giants, trophies of victory, tombs of shepherds, asylums for the living, watchtowers, prisons, and temples for the worship of fire, of religious or mystic festivals, or of the gods themselves; they may have originated in Phoenicia, Greece, the Orient or Atlantis.

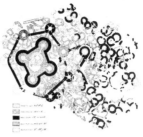

Nuraghe Barumini began as a tower and expanded into a village.

The general position is that they served as protection from raiders and pirates, yet most *nuraghe* can barely house a dozen people comfortably, with little space for food storage, no allowance for sewage, and no access to potable water. In the case of towers designed with a single chamber, in which four people constitutes a crowd, living conditions would have been both impractical and intolerable. Half a dozen soldiers would have easily laid siege and starved its occupants in no time at all. They are useless as defenses, and the enormous effort required just to protect a handful of individuals far outweighs the benefit. So this view is also wanting. However, historians do have a point in cases where the structures have grown organically from a single to a multi-purpose compound, incorporating as many as twenty-one towers joined by internal courtyards, the Sardinian version of Lego. And they finally incorporated a really useful feature: a well. Obviously these are more likely to have been used as communal fortifications, even if the majority of adjacent structures are found *outside* the defensive wall. Barumini, one of the largest complexes, began as a single tower and gradually expanded into a fortification by 1270 BC. It too leaves the majority of extended habitations outside the fortress wall, offering little to no sense of security.[25]

The impression we are left with is of a redevelopment of the sites as the culture adapted to changing times and needs. Aristotle probably came closest to the mark, at least in spirit, when he remarked, "it is said that in the island of Sardinia are edifices of the ancients, erected after the Greek manner, and many other beautiful buildings, and [domes] finished in excellent proportions,"[26] and since Greek architecture has its origins in Asia Minor and Scythia, the essence of Aristotle's remark may yet prove constructive to our quest.

No matter where in the world you travel, memories of parallel ancient civilizations are slow to fade, and among Sardinia's enduring folklore there are useful insights into the nature of the *nuraghe*. Luigi Muscas recorded a few: "The *nuraghe* were designed and built by people who came from the sky, thanks to their high degree of evolution... They showed new techniques and unknown materials to the local people, such as kneaded stone, where the shredded stone is mingled with sand and fragments of animals, thus in many stone blocks there appear animal footprints, left when the dough was still fresh. The towers represented the mirror of constellations on the ground. Through their perforated tops they received the corresponding celestial energy. This is why we can say that the giant people were in direct connection with the divine. But the *nuraghe* were also linked to each other, they functioned as spiritual communicators and especially for a harmonious coexistence within the cosmic

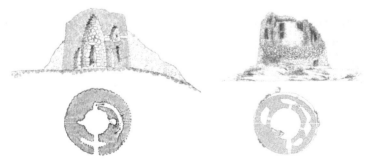

Nuraghe Nura. And Dun Carloway, Isle of Lewis.

and divine law... They were also physically linked by tunnels. When I was fifteen I saw one at the S'ununcu of de Sensu. However, returning thirty years later, I noticed that it had been obstructed by large boulders."[27]

Further enquiries on the origin of *nuraghe*, this time at the Archaeological Museum in Cagliari, produced opinions, educated guesses and shrugs, but no conclusive answers. "It's a mystery."

The more *nuraghe* I examined the more it dawned on me that I'd seen this type of building before: at Dun Carloway on the Isle of Lewis, and in more ruined states throughout Orkney. Same design, same architecture. And just as some *nuraghe* were later developed and expanded into places of habitation and protection, so were the *duns* (or *brochs* as they are sometimes called), some of which incorporated basements and cisterns, and yet they still remain as alien to Scotland as *nuraghe* are to Sardinia, but between the two there is obviously a connection. The problem was that hardly anyone was looking in the Mediterranean. Given the recurring references to Orion and the folklore about the towers being mirrors of constellations, I wondered if the same sky-ground relationship might also be at play here.

I drove with Paola, Regina and a small camera crew to the central highlands to examine the well-preserved Nuraghe Ruju, situated on a plain with an unrestrained view of the horizon. At this point neither the crew nor I were familiar with stories of the towers being receptors of telluric current, and yet we all felt it; one cameraman was visually transformed by the experience, and the emotional impact was to stay with him for months to come.

One is aware of a presence, a being, a welcoming one at that. Speaking of their own experiences, local villagers remarked: "one sees them but they do not let themselves be touched."[28]

Walking up to the second level at Ruju one comes to a beehive chamber facing a narrow window set into the exterior wall; a niche in the rear of the chamber misaligns with the window, narrowing the field of vision to a specific hill whose summit has been artificially flattened, as though creating a focal point for an object in the sky. Had I been watching the stars from this position on the winter solstice in the era of 6000 BC, I would have witnessed Orion's Belt rising dramatically out of that summit. To the east of the hill, a second artificial summit serves as a platform for the rising of Sirius.

Suddenly, the *nuraghe* were starting to look less like fortifications and more like observational instruments.

A few minutes' drive southwest, with windshield wipers in full motion, we arrived at Nuraghe Santu Antine. The large conical tower was later extended into a triangular enclosure made of thick walls, into which

Nuraghe Ruju.

148

are set various habitations. Two wells were dug inside the newly formed courtyard; later still a wider perimeter wall was added as a defensive measure, but set so low that the occupants it was designed to protect presumably were killed by anxiety.

The entrance to the original central tower leads to a tall beehive chamber featuring side rooms arranged in a cloverleaf pattern not dissimilar to the design of Maltese temples. Its narrow window also offers an unobstructed view of the horizon and another artificially flattened summit, out of which the winter solstice Sun would have been observed rising c.7000 BC. However, the same summit also allows for the descent of Orion's Belt and Sirius in 6000 BC, completing the trajectory first observed up the road at Nuraghe Ruju. Essentially the two towers work together to mark the motion of two notable objects in the sky on the same date.

This correlation must have been of great importance to Sardinians of the period because the identical reference appears two hundred years earlier at Nuraghe Niedu, and five hundred years earlier still at three other loca-

Beehive chamber. Nuraghe Ruju.

tions: Pira 'e Zuri at Losa, Is Paras, and Corbos a Silanus. The latter features an uncomfortably small entrance and a tiny light box in its interior chamber as though maintaining darkness was of

Sa Coveccada.

paramount importance, just as it was among astronomical observatories throughout the ancient world.

The oldest date reference so far comes from Nuraghe Barumini, whose original tower marks both Orion and Sirius at mid-heaven on the winter solstice in 7300 BC.

I was almost starting to enjoy getting drenched.

I gleaned over my notes on the Orcadian stone circles and the time when they reflected the three stars of Orion's Belt in 5300 BC. Might the ancient architects have memorialized the same relationship here earlier? Looking

Nuraghe Ruju.
Window allows a sightline
to a flattened hill.

at the map of the Sardinian highlands, there indeed was a third site nearby, not a tower but a dolmen (a rarity in Sardinia) by the name Sa Coveccada. A close inspection, however, shows the stones to be the passage chamber of what was once a formidable passage mound.

Barely five miles apart, these three sites form a straight line, with the third site offset by 2°, altogether mimicking the belt stars of Orion at their mid-heaven position in the era of

150

6000 BC. Even the belt's incline relative to the horizon is echoed on the ground. And just as the circle and stone chamber of Bookan differs from the other two on Orkney, so Sa Coveccada in Sardinia is the odd one out.

Sa Coveccada may have served a dual function. The complete loss of soil cover, along with significant damage to the portal stones has necessitated extensive rebuilding. Based on direct observation, it seems as though the original alignment may be off by as much as 5°. As it stands, its orientation matches the rising of Orion's Belt in the era of 2600 BC, and while this may pose a conundrum with respect to my hypothesis, there is a precedent. When Robert Bauval and Adrian Gilbert published their thesis proving a mirroring between Orion's Belt and the three Giza pyramids in 10,450 BC,[29] they also discovered that the Great Pyramid's shafts reference stars of four significant constellations in a second era, 2450 BC. Could it be that people well versed in astronomy, and borrowing from the same manual, created a similar double-reference at Sa Coveccada? Perhaps, but at the very least I now had a direct relationship between the astronomer architects of Sardinia and Scotland.

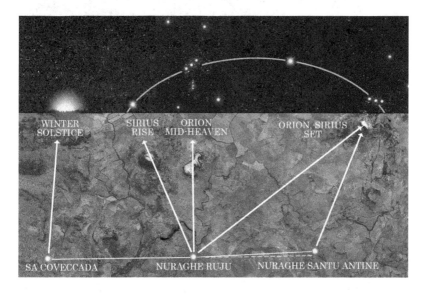

The plains in the immediate vicinity of Nuraghe Santu Antine are dotted with other towers, along with a number of unspecified monuments that fell to the modern tractor and plough. The region reminded me of the pastoral landscape of southern Britain, a land brimming with ancient sites of veneration, legends of faeries and giants, and orbs descending from the sky to follow the farmers. In the years I lived there I assisted in mapping hundreds of sites that mirror specific constellations, with temples such as Avebury and Stonehenge corresponding to Draco as it appeared in 2600 BC. Taking the folklore recorded by Luigi Muscas at face value, and using Nuraghe Santu Antine as a focal point, when the surrounding towers are plotted on a map they form the mirror image of the seven sisters of the Pleiades,[30] meaning that ancient

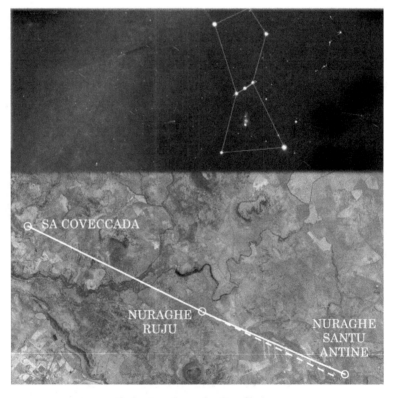

Orion's mirror in Sardinia.

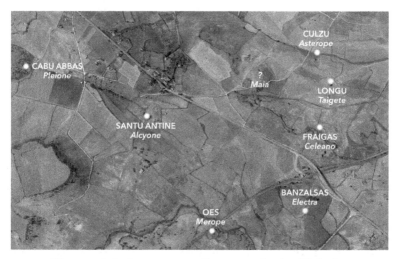

Sites and their corresponding stars in the Pleiades.

Sardinians followed the sky-ground symbolism practiced by ancient Egyptians. If one allows for the eighth star, Maia, its position matches a square mound topped by a thick limestone wall of what appears to have been a step pyramid. Although the site has yet to be properly investigated, its general alignment points once more to the rising of Orion and Sirius on the winter solstice c.6000 BC.

Approaching the village of Las Plassas, the brakes were applied hard. The hill ahead had a perfectly conical, man-made demeanor despite the best efforts to conceal it with conifers and a castle on top. Pyramids may sound out of place in Sardinia yet just about everyone knows about them. From the assembled eyewitness accounts, there once existed pyramids near the towns of Sa Contissa, S'Arriu de sa Prua and Corte Baccasa.[31] Some, like the one in the province of Sassari, were of the stepped variety; others are so old that erosion and sediment reveal only the tip,[32] while many more had their stone pillaged for building material, often at the behest of priests compelled to curtail the devil's real estate empire, coincidentally at the same time that monetary donations were made to their own.[33]

To transport this much stone would have originally required a sizeable and organized society, and certainly the memory of lost cities remains deeply embedded in local traditions, as a stop for coffee and conversation in any village will reveal. One individual, Alfredo Garau, recalls the site of an ancient lost city in the area of Is Cappelas: "This legend tells of a highly evolved people, noble people, who came from the sky 10,000 years ago. Here, on the plateau of the country, was built a city of 10,000 inhabitants... These people had a fleet of 1200 ships with which it sailed around the world to spread its civilization and knowledge. The location? My family landed in the region of Sa Contissa and it was there that my father and I unearthed ancient walls three or four meters thick. We did not know at the time the value of this discovery... Since we farmers do not follow linguistic "contaminations" of Spanish and Italian, we continue to use the term *arba*, our ancient word and the same one that gave the name to the vanished city."[34]

Pyramid of Las Plassas.

Sardinia's monumental ancestry continues to vanish at a monumental pace, yet creeping urbanization sometimes helps uncover a hidden world. Towards the highlands, not far from a tomb of the faeries on the outskirts of the town of Mamoaida, building work at a bed and breakfast uncovered a series of carved stones. One menhir, estimated to have been carved in 3500 BC (although the date is pure guesswork), is eleven feet tall and covered in circles, ripples and lines forming seven pictograms. In form and design the pictograms are identical to those found throughout the western coast of Scotland, specifically at Cairnbaan and Achnabreck in Kilmartin Glen. The symbols resemble the tracks of protons and neutrons photographed in particle chambers, but from another perspective they could also be maps of the sky – it is one of those on-going mysteries. The other being, did this stone carver take his art to Scotland?

Sardinia stillhad one more ace up its sleeve. In between drizzle and drenchings I followed the gang, led by our interpreter Rosalia, to see Domus de Janas Salixi, a sacred site off the beaten track. It was definitely out of the ordinary, like the weather that day – the Sun was finally allowed out for good behavior. An oval limestone dome protruded from a shallow valley with a stream, exposed to the sky out of lichen and grass like an expectant belly.

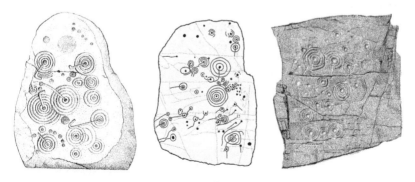

Mamoaida stone, and comparative art in Scotland.

Domus de Janas Salixi.

Five small, separate entrances, expertly incised into the curving incline, lead into individual crawl spaces, each with two to three chambers, low of ceiling and barely large enough for three people to sit comfortably, each chamber separated by a raised picture frame-style border. Tradition refers to the location as a sacred retreat for women undergoing initiation, and instruction on fertility and birthing, in its many interpretations. As one would expect, the chambers make one feel as though immersed inside wombs.

A brief shower vied with the Sun as I crawled my way inside, to be greeted with a distinct sense of déjà-vu: I was back inside Dwarfie Stane on the island of Hoy. The chamber even carries the same difficult, low pitch resonance, hardly surprising since the priestesses of old hummed in a very low tone whenever they conducted rituals. There was no mistaking it, whoever carved these chambers had their work duplicated in that distant Orcadian valley, right down to the architectural features. And that unnerving sound.

Yet another link between these two separate islands.

Back in Cagliari, sitting in the patio of Antico Caffè, a delightful turn of the century bistro I'd commandeered as a temporary office, I was assisted in my notes by a dissatisfaction of not knowing the origin or meaning of *nuraghe*. I was about to concede defeat, yet the odd references to Asia Minor and Malta made me wonder whether the term had migrated westwards across the Mediterranean, just like the myriad of cultures who settled here.

A day's sailing south and around Sicily, Malta shares much in common with Sardinia. It is home to a unique Neolithic temple culture, with the forecourts of the temples of Mnadra, Hagar Qim and Ggantija featuring the same horned design and, just as in Sardinia, long stripped of soil cover. Each one is astronomically aligned, with Ggantija's double entrance referencing the winter solstice and the Lunar Standstill in 12,000 BC, made possible by artificially flattening a nearby hill.[35] Legends are adamant that the megalithic architects of Malta were very tall or giant people,[36] and like Sardinia, a significant portion of the population once had dolichocephalic skulls, proved

Any resemblance to Dwarfie Stane is purely deliberate.

157

when excavation of a hypogeum at Hal Safflieni uncovered thousands of such people unceremoniously buried in this man-made underground labyrinth – although 'dumped' is more appropriate, because the manner in which skulls, skeletons, animals and household utensils where interred is consistent with a huge tidal wave sweeping over the island, forcing everything in its path into every available orifice. The discovery implies that Malta too was once home to a secluded priesthood, or at the very least a people who looked and behaved differently to regular inhabitants.[37]

With the lowest habitation layer at the temple of Tarxien estimated at 8000 BC, and at this point predating Sardinia,[38] we can speculate that whoever was in charge of Malta's temple culture took their know-how and sailed north. But what might this have to do with a nuragic culture?

For the most part, ancient Malta was colonized and influenced by people migrating from the direction of Asia Minor, and this is reflected in its language, an amalgam of Arabic, Hebrew, Near Eastern, Indo-European and North African. Although the showcase temple Hagar Qim means 'worshiping stones' in Maltese, the Armenian root words *hay-kar-kimia* mean 'alchemical Armenian stones'. Since *hayk* also refers to the constellation Orion, the phrase can also be interpreted as 'alchemical stones of Orion', and indeed the constellation would have been observed from this temple's southerly entrance when it rose out of the Mediterranean on the winter solstice in 5600 BC.

In Maltese language we also find the word *nur*. It means 'just or rightful people'. Its root lies in Azerbaijan (what used to be old Armenia) where it means 'light or shining', while the root of *aghe – ag –* means 'white'. Thus *nur-ag* are 'white, shining, just or rightful people', what

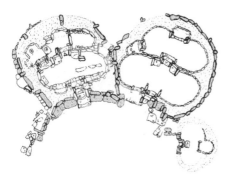

Mnajdra temple complex.

appears to be a description of the Shining Ones. Classical Armenian language offers specific details about these rightful people. The word *nuirag* refers to 'a holy representative or legate', from which comes *nuiryal*, 'devoted'; its derivative *nuiragan* refers to something sacred or divine.

Altogether, *nuraghe* are best described as places of 'the rightful, white, shining, holy representatives', and given their ineffectiveness as defensive buildings, the idea of *nuraghe* as restricted places of assembly for a close-knit class of astronomer priests now makes practical sense.[39]

In an added twist, *nur'* is the Armenian word for pomegranate. Aside from the passing visual association between the textured wall of the towers and the pomegranate seeds attached to their mesocarp, there appears to be no connection whatsoever between the two, but on closer inspection it may just tie all these threads together.

In remote times, the Armenian Highlands were home to the Subari people, whose high degree of skills from architecture to metallurgy became the foundation for an anomalous civilization that spread southwards into Mesopotamia – the Sumerian.[40] Large limestone panels with carved reliefs found at the Sumerian city of Nimrud depict groups of *apkallu* (sages) holding a bag in one hand, and in the other a *mullilu*, a 'tree fruit'. A close look at the *apkallu* beside the Tree of Knowledge shows these anthropomorphic individuals picking fruit from a flowering variety of shrub, and the one that best fits the description throughout the Middle East is the pomegranate tree. But what makes the pomegranate so important?

"About the pomegranate I must say nothing," whispered the 2nd century geographer Pausanias, "for its story is somewhat of a holy mystery." And he was right. In symbolism and mythology, the pomegranate represents the point of contact between this world and that of the gods. In the Greek mythological story of Persephone, for example, it is used as a metaphor of spiritual rebirth and the cycle of nature, because after Persephone marries the god Hades, she is given six pomegranate seeds as her only source of nutrition during her six months in the Otherworld. In a comparative myth, Orion is wedded to Side, whose name means 'pomegranate'. Since this myth is based on the older story of Osiris, whom the Egyptians identified with Orion, a link is established between this tree fruit and the resurrected hero. The pomegranate plant and its fruit were respected in Greek and earlier Zoroastrian resurrection rituals as the sacred plant inhabiting Eden. Since the plant is evergreen, it naturally became a figurative representation of the immortality of the soul, which, after all, is the prime objective of the initiate undertaking a death-and-rebirth ritual. This analogy is elegantly exemplified in Persian mythology by the hero Isfandiyar, who eats a pomegranate and becomes invincible.

The *Apkallu* represented a learned elite that shared its wisdom with the curious, whereby any ordinary individual was required to 'eat' the fruit from the Tree of Knowledge in order to journey into the Otherworld and return as a god.[41] It is tempting to see the *nuraghe* and its associated culture in Sardinia forming part of this expanding cult of wisdom, with the towers serving as metaphoric receptacles where secret traditions were conveyed to a select few, a continuation of Mysteries schools stemming from Mesopotamia and its parent culture in the Armenian Highlands.

A linguistic link exists between these ideas. In remote times when the kingdoms of Urartu and Armenia were indistinguishable, the Sun god Ara was also called Ardi, from which derives the namesake culture Ur-Ardi and Ur-artu ('land of the Sun'). Ara's wife was

An Apkallu picks a pomegranate.

Nu-ard, 'bride of the Sun', referring to the Sun's companion, the Moon. This goddess was also called Sel-ardi,[42] and as the name migrated into the Mediterranean it took on the shorthand form S'ardi, as in 'belonging to Ardi', from which developed the country named Sardinia, the 'land of the bride of the Sun'.

And so it is that in the Land of the Bride of the Sun we find horned mounds, stone towers, recurring associations with Orion and Sirius, giants, an ecumenical group behaving differently from ordinary citizens, experts in astronomy, masonry and seafaring: the very elements underpinning the sacred landscape of distant Orkney and the Islands of the Brides.

To this growing list we can also add etymology. Take the anomalous stone tower north of Callanish, Dun Carloway. Officially the name derives from the Norse *Karlavag*, 'Karl's bay', or its derivative *kar-vayr*, a stone-room, and at first glance this seems to be a satisfactory explanation. But with Norse being an extension of old Germanic which in turn derives from Indo-European originating in the Armenian Highlands, we might entertain the following suggestions, courtesy of the Armenian language: *dun* (dwelling), and *dohm* (a noble race or family); and Carloway: *kar* (stone), *ogh* (ring or circle) and *e'ag* (being, existence), creating Dun Kar-ogh-e'ag, purportedly meaning 'existence of the circular stone dwelling of a family of noble race'.

There is obviously a pattern developing here between the megalithic cultures of Scotland and Sardinia with ties to a parent culture in Armenia. And not just linguistically, but also stylistically. For example, at the nuragic complex of S'Arcu 'e Is Forros – once an important metallurgical center trading with the eastern Mediterranean – stone blocks belonging to a Neolithic structure reveal stylized faces sculpted in relief that are carbon copies of a standing stone uncovered at the religious center of Artsakh in Armenia.

Two pieces of circumstantial evidence point to a migration from Armenia to the Mediterranean, and from there to the northern extremes of Europe. Geneticists scanned the genomes of Armenians and found them to be a mix of ancient populations whose descendants live in Sardinia today. These same people are closely linked to Neolithic farmers who brought agriculture to Europe around 6000 BC.[43] This was a period in flux, with the Earth warming from the collapse of the Younger Dryas ice age, and the practical needs of people adapting every generation to survive and maintain permanent societies. The abrupt drainage of Laurentide lakes in North America and the associated rapid switch of the North Atlantic ocean's thermohaline circulation c.6200 BC had a catastrophic influence on Neolithic civilization in large parts of south-eastern Europe, Asia Minor, Cyprus, and the Near East. The event triggered disastrous tsunami and raised sea levels by twelve feet, drowning coastal lands, including Orkney. The abrupt decrease in temperatures led to a prolonged drought that caused a widespread die-off of fauna,[44] followed by a thousand years of high rainfall before shifting to dryer spells again in 5500 BC.[45] The eastern Mediterranean experienced the brunt of this cocktail of instability.[46] It would have made any sensible person migrate long distances in search of a stable environment. These scenarios and their relative dates fit remarkably well with the archaeoastronomical dates for the temples established on Sardinia, and later on Orkney.

With so many connections between Sardinia and Scotland now steering us towards Asia Minor and the Armenian Highlands, perhaps we ought to look eastwards and see what more we can learn about these ancient wandering architects.

Carvings at S'Arcu 'e Is Forros and Artsakh.

Stones of the Ancient Garments. Ceann Hulavig.

THE SECRET MEMORY
OF WORDS

hen written history, oral legend, symbol or folklore are lacking, absence of information can be restored by <u>examining the origin</u> of words and their <u>relationship to the land.</u> The names of places in ancient times derived from the observation of local topography, events, ritual practices, and, with regard to monuments, their associated activity, function and purpose. In a manner of speaking, names functioned as mnemonic devices for the foreign visitor or the absent minded.

For pilgrims of the distant future such as ourselves, they illuminate and clarify our surroundings. For example, should you visit the Isle of Lewis and ask directions to Cnoc a Ruagain, you will hear, "Ach, yer lookin' fa 'the hill from which sheep are driven far and wide in summer'?" Because that's precisely what it means. Or how about Griomastra, 'a low dark place with hills between it and the evening Sun'. And should you be searching for 'the rock beside the loch with a breach in the middle' you'd best follow the sign to Sgaravat. Anglicization, although useful to non-Gaelic speakers, has distorted the linguistic landscape, so when you order fish n' chips in Orkney's main town of Kirkwall you are at the same time standing in the old Norse town Kirkavå and the Gaelic Bàgh na h-Eaglaise.

Most place names throughout Orkney and the Outer Hebrides are Gaelic in origin, yet there is always the unmistakable influence of Scandinavian, whose own roots trace back a further 5000 years to Ukraine, Greece, and Armenia.[1] Unfortunately, due to humanity's annoying habit of refusing to sit still, migration makes it difficult to pinpoint when a name might have come into existence, but at least it provides context.

The hypothesis that Orkney and the Western Isles were only settled by Scandinavians around 700 AD is now redundant, thanks in part to the discovery of human artefacts dating to Mesolithic times. Surely the earliest settlers must have assigned names to local features and monuments using their native tongues? Support for this appears in *Ravenna Cosmography,* a text preceding the Nordic migration to Orkney, in which it is mentioned that the various groups of islanders knew the same islands in the archipelago by different names, so much so that when Scandinavian settlement began in earnest, the outsiders came face-to-face with three languages already in use, to which they added their own.[2]

Gaelic languages, although mainly associated with Scotland, Wales and Ireland, also fall under the wider Indo-European language family, with close relationships to Celtiberian, Gaulish, and the distant Egyptian, Scythian and Armenian tongues. Estimates for the emergence of proto-Gaelic in Ireland vary widely, from the introduction of agriculture c.7000 BC to around the first centuries BC. Little can be said with certainty, as the language now known as Old Irish only began to be properly recorded with the Christianization of the island in the 4th century and the introduction of Roman script. Even Celtic and Germanic languages are developments of older root languages from the east, regions such as India, Mesopotamia, Siberia, and principally the lands bordering the Black and Caspian seas generally referred to as the Armenian Highlands. This is why, during the compilation of the Armenian-German dictionary, more than a thousand identical word roots and participles were revealed between the two.[3]

Among Indo-European languages, Armenian stands alone. It is closer to Greek and Iranian and has been a spoken language in the Armenian Highlands and surrounding territories since at least 7500 BC.[4] Its flow into Europe most likely began with migrations around the same era, a hypothesis matched by genetic studies proving that early soil cultivators migrated from Asia Minor.[5]

To expect words to remain unchanged for millennia is asking for the impossible, their phonology changes through cultural diffusion, dialect, alphabet, writing, translation, transliteration and topography. Furthermore the geographic movement of language alters the way consonants are pronounced by adjacent cultures, generating local variations of identical words. A dweller in any given land may find difficulty inflecting introduced words, like Japanese people rolling an 'R', or non-Arabic people forming the guttural throat stop common to Arabic speech, as in *h-eh*. In the same way, words with *v* are elsewhere spoken with a softer *b*, just as the sounds *h, k and g* are often interchangeable. The same applies to vowels. There are countless examples of Armenian loan words exported across national boundaries with altered spellings but with meanings intact, for example, city names in Urartia and Sumeria, where *Ar* becomes *Ur*, *Aridou* becomes *Erridu*, and *Nipar* becomes *Nippour*.[6]

As Armenian language migrated deeper into western Europe it served as the root for Gothic, Anglo-Saxon, Basque, Breton and Gaelic/Welsh vocabulary. Take the Armenian word for wool, *gel-mn*, that has been retained in Breton, Cornish and Welsh as *gloan, gluan* and *gwan* respectively. Due to regional linguistic and phonetic variations, *g* is often replaced by *v* and *w*, resulting in the Gothic *vulla*, the Czech *vluna*, the Dutch *wol*, and finally the Anglo-Saxon variant, *wull*.[7]

In looking for the origin of ancient place names it is therefore important not to read them literally but phonetically, and to pay attention to enunciation – to the rhythmic dance between vowels and consonants. When asking a Norwegian if she's traveling to 'Shetland', for instance, until your tongue performs the acute gymnastics required to make the word come out as *Hjaltland* (the earlier Norse name for the archipelago) she won't understand what you're trying to communicate.

Throughout previous chapters I have been suggesting a possible Armenian origin for names such as *nuraghe*, which originates from *nuirag*, 'a holy representative or legate'; or Sardinia, from *s'ardi*, 'land of the bride of the Sun'. Without expectation I decided to look into the origin of every place name we've encountered so far to see how deep the influence of Armenian language might have been in ancient Scotland, because it might just lead to the source of those ancient architects and stargazers.

Of course this also meant coming to grips with a rare yet profoundly influential ancient tongue.

In his tome *On The Ocean*, written around 325 BC, the Greek geographer Pytheas of Massalia mentions the islands at the extreme end of Britain as *Orkas*. Given the influence of Old Norse in Orkney it is reasonable to assume the name comes from the noun *orka*, meaning 'strength, power, energy', yet none of these terms adequately describe the land – unless, of course, Vikings were psychic and foresaw the future use of wind and wave turbines in which Orkney now leads the world. The verb *orka å*, 'to influence or affect someone', is equally unsatisfying, so perhaps the name carries an earlier fingerprint.

Armenian presents several possibilities. The best fit, *Ar-kar-negh*, translates as 'narrow stones of the god', aptly describing the physical characteristics of the stones of Stenness, or the way the circles track the motions of the stars, which back in the day were considered gods, living entities in their own right. Its variant, *Ar-kar-nakh*, 'principal stones of the god', also seems befitting.

A third possibility, *orenkn-e,* translates as 'it is the law', implying a landscape where the perpetual harmony of the heavens was mirrored in the temples so as to establish a terrestrial order. By extension, inhabitants came under the jurisdiction of divine rules that assisted greater congruity with the environment and, in theory, helped them lead a balanced existence. This fundamental concept lies at the core of the world's most ancient temple cities.

Without doubt, the main feature of Orkney is the row of three breathtaking stone circles. Bookan may no longer look as magnificent now that its stones have been pillaged and its central chamber lies in ruins, but it does occupy the highest point along the isthmus and marks the tail end of the Orion alignment. The description of the site is expressed in Armenian as *poch'-gah*, 'tail throne', and *poch'-karer,* 'tail stones'.

The middle stone circle is the Ring of Brodgar, or as it was earlier spelled, Broggar, a corruption of the Scandinavian *bru-gard* meaning 'bridge enclosure', a fair description of its location near the short bridge between two lochs. This much was true in the era of the Scandinavians, however the lochs are the result of rising sea levels. In the era the circle was built, Loch Stenness was little more than a narrow outlet for Loch Harray and easily forded on foot. Of the three circles, Brodgar is the only one commemorated by the legend of giants dancing to music and turned to stone. In this respect the Armenian phrase *barerq-kar* comes closer to the mark, for it means 'dance song stones'. I thought this was satisfactory, until one day, while having coffee and *namoura* (an ancient Egyptian-style honey cake) by the Nile and consulting E.A. Wallis Budge's *Egyptian Hieroglyphic Dictionary,* I was surprised to come across the compound word *b-ra-gah,* literally 'abode or shrine of the Sun god'. This is about as close as one can get phonetically to Broggar, and adequately describes the circle's astronomical function as a solar observatory. If so then we are looking at an overlap of two of the most ancient languages on this remote island.

How plausible could this be? Consider that pharaoh Mena (also spelled Min), ascended the Egyptian throne c.3113 BC as the "first pharaoh of a purely human blood-line,"[8] yet may have been of Armenian descent, given that the Armenian title *Minas* means 'first great man'. And his isn't the only example. Pharaonic names such as Tuthmosis, Amenhotep and Ramesses also have Armenian transliterations.[9]

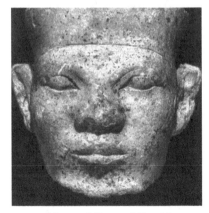

Egyptian territory and influence once spread far into Upper Mesopotamia, bordering and overlapping the Armenian Highlands, hence why it has been

Mena, Min or Minas?

convincingly argued that the land of Ermenen mentioned by Thutmosis III is a linguistic variant of Armenia; the Egyptologist Flinders Petrie speculated that Queen Tii herself was of Armenian/ Mitannian origin, and that it was she who brought the Aten cult to Egypt, teaching it to her son Akhenaten.[10] In turn, his wife Nefertiti, whose name in Armenian means 'she who became the backbone

Nefertiti. Potentially of Armenian origin.

of the ruler', has also been suspected of being of northern origin, due in part to her bust clearly depicting a woman who defined Caucasian female beauty. A letter penned by Nefertiti to her father asks him to send precious metals down "from the northern country" as part of her dowry, and since the only country bordering northern Egypt at the time was Armenian territory, there is substance to this hypothesis.[11]

Expectations for the third site, Stenness (Stenis in its older spelling) were pretty high, and thankfully the Armenian language did not disappoint. With its colossal linear slabs, Stenness stands apart from the others, a unique personality. Anyone who has stood in its shadow intuitively feels this to be a seat of status and is instantly elevated by it. We find these qualities reflected in the phrase *tses-nisd*, 'seat of ritual'. Its variant *S'tenel-nish*, means 'to place a mark'.

Once again, ancient Egyptian language adds fuller interpretations, as the following three examples demonstrate: *s-ten-nes* (to arrive at a distinguished place); *seh-t-en-nes* (to approach a place of council); and *set-em-*

nes (connected stone throne tail). All three hit the mark. From these emerges the variant *stenit* (sovereignty).[12]

As these examples illustrate, there is no doubt as to the additional presence of Egyptian words and phrases on Orkney, just as they are on the archipelago halfway to Iceland, the Faroe Islands. It has been suggested [13] that the name Faroe itself stems from *per-åa*, 'praised seat of government'.[14] There is an extension of this term and it applies to a key stellar relationship that has cropped up throughout this odyssey: the term *per-Åa-t* reads 'seat of government of the Kingdom of Osiris'.[15] As we already know, this god is the earthly embodiment of Orion, whom the Egyptians named *Sahu*. Sahu, and the star it leads, Sirius, was used as a seasonal marker for cultivation. This quality is reflected in the Faroese word *saa*, which means 'to sow'.[16] Likewise the Egyptian concept of *nw* (the primordial ocean from which all life emanates) is reflected in the Faeroese word for 'spring or fountain', *nu*.[17]

Overlooking the Orkney circles from its higher elevation, the passage mound Maeshowe resembles a place of gathering, of council. It is

Stenness, the Place of Council.

unusual insofar as it celebrates the descent rather than ascent of three celestial gods – Sun, Moon and Orion – as though the people who assembled here did so in preparation to cross a metaphoric boundary. There are several possible interpretations in Armenian: *marz-ar* (province or domain of the god), *marz-hayel* (to look into a province or domain), and *marz-haverz* (eternal province or domain),

Each is entirely plausible, given the relationship between the mound and the descent of a 'god' into a province or domain known to the Gaels as Annwn and to Egyptians as Amdwat.

I believe there is an even more compelling option. *Marz-hay* (pronounced *mes-hui*) translates as 'province of the Armenians'; taken at face value the phrase defines both the mound and the region as the domain of a group of migrating individuals. Given what we learned earlier about the early inhabitants of Orkney, the Papae, whose name comes from *p'apegh*, the Armenian term for a monk or holy person, the hypothesis is compelling, made all the stronger by the relationship between the movement of Neolithic people from eastern Europe between 6000-5000 BC which coincides with the dates memorialized by the Orkney sites. But there's more behind *Marz-hay* and it requires an understanding of how the gods came to define a people.

The indigenous god of the Armenian Highlands is Ara, who represents the rejuvenation of nature and lends his name to a region called Ar-me-ni, the 'land of the sons of Ar'.[18] Contemporary with Ara is the curly-haired, sparkly-eyed god Hayk (pronounced *huy*), who is ultimately raised to heaven where he becomes as a star, the mighty archer Orion.[19]

Together, Hayk and Ara define the sacred foundation. And while Ara came to define the land, Hayk defined its people, hence Armenians refer to themselves as Hay or Hayk, 'people of Orion'.[20]

Let's now put this in context of Orkney and Maeshowe. With *marz-hay* we are offered two interpretations: 'province of Orion' and 'province of the people of Orion'. However, the similar word *mes* means 'great or noble', providing a third possibility, *mes-hayk*, 'noble people of Orion'.

By bringing the god Ara into the equation, the possibilities expand. Depending on the context, the root *ar* can mean 'assembly', 'creation that connects to light', 'nobility', 'power' and 'sun'.[21] We can therefore take the variant *mes-ar* to mean 'great assembly of nobility' or 'great assembly of the sun'.

Placing this in context of the mound and its encircling water-bearing ditch, contemporary proto-Celt temple tradition defines a sacred place as *nemos*, and in Gaulish and Brittonic as *nemeton*, meaning 'sky ground', a meeting place between two planes of existence otherwise known as the middle ground. Such *nemeton* were typically surrounded by a bank and a ditch filled with water, defining the sacred area of the gods as a place of council.[22]

Realistically, we do not know which linguist form gave rise to Maeshowe, but this overlapping of proto-Celt temple tradition and Armenian etymology offers a clear picture of a mound associated with the Sun and used as a place of select assembly by a specific group of people who were culturally defined by Orion.

To add an Egyptian spin, the compound word *mes-hau* means 'to be born or produced from a temple',[23] but since Maeshowe does not conform to the traditional elements defining a birthing house (for this the mound would need to be oriented east or south-east), the phrase could be applied symbolically. If so, then Maeshowe can be defined as a place of ceremony from which an ordinary person emerged as a noble.

I am confident there is enough circumstantial evidence here to link the ancient architects of Orkney with the Armenian Highlands, and to some degree Egypt, so we'll seal this inquiry with two more examples. The horned passage mound of Work is accurately described by the Armenian *v-orc'*, 'a den, burrow or covert', while the effulgent, mountainous island of Hoy, with its Sardinian-style sandstone chamber, arises from *hoyaoab*, 'high, magnificent', or simply *hayk* or its diminutive *hy*, referring to the island as the point of reference for the rising and setting of Orion, exactly as observed from Maeshowe and its three attendant stone circles.

Turning our attention to the Outer Hebrides, we have already established these Hy Bryges to mean 'domain of noble Armenians of Orion'.

The largest island in the chain comprises the lowlands of Lewis and the mountains of Harris. Under the Armenian magnifying glass, Lewis couldn't be more straightforward: *luys* means 'light'. As for Harris, or *harit*, it is the 'place of Sun worshippers',[24] which may sound like sarcasm, given the weather, yet before climate change took hold of the region and forced people onto mainland Scotland, the Hebrides were far more predisposed to a sunny and temperate climate. In any event, this is not the kind of 'sun' they came to worship – they could have stayed in the Mediterranean for that.

Looking across to Harris from the lochs and moors of Lewis.

Metaphorically the island may have been a land to where a spiritual people traveled to find 'light' and 'sun' in the context of enlightenment and nature worship, which satisfies both the folklore and the context of the stone circles.

If so, then the idea that the nine-stone circle Ceann Hulavig once served as a seat reserved for white-robed wisdom keepers fits well with three potential Armenian sources: *halav-vagh* (ancient garment), *halav-veh* (majestic garment), and *halav-varg* ('garment of esteemed name'). Together *kar halav-vagh* marks the 'stones of the ancient garments'. A more obscure title by which the stone circle is known in Gaelic, *Sron A'chail*,[25] may originate from *srah achk-aha*, 'the room of seeing', in effect identifying this stone circle as a location used by a select group who undertook vision quests.

The focal point of Lewis is undoubtedly the near-perfectly preserved stone circle and cruciform avenues at Callanish. The summit of its teardrop ridge is marked by a rocky outcrop called Clach An Tursa, where a number of massive stones once stood. Here the Armenian term *tur' sar* literally means 'door or gateway to the summit'.

As for Callanish, both the word and its pronunciation remain almost intact in Armenian: *kar-nish*, 'a stone

Summit of the Stone Doorway. Callanish.

176

marker'. Its variants are *kharag-nish*, 'rock cliff marker', and *khachanish*, 'to mark or cross'.

There is also the derivative *khardeash*, meaning 'fair or light-skinned', a potential reference to the physical appearance of the 'shining one', the light-skinned priest who once performed ceremonies here. Another derivative *karanai* ('I am turned to stone'), might also apply, seeing as it echoes the legends of the stones as petrified priests.

Gaelic people gave this location a secondary name, Tursachan ('standing stones'), and it is still used in signs directing visitors to the site. Its probable Armenian origin is quite explicit: *tur'sa-qah*, 'doorway to the stone seat or throne'; or even *tur'-sar-kar*, 'summit of the stone doorway'. A visiting Egyptian might expand on this by adding that *Ta Ur s-àqer* means 'to make perfect the great land of gods'. And if this doesn't impress, he might go a step further with *Ta Ur s-àten*, 'transfer from the Sun god to perfect the great land of the gods'.[26] That's quite a promise.

Obviously this sacred place was of considerable importance as a focal center of spirituality, community and learning, its function maintained well into historic times by the white-robed Druidhe, whose presence is commemorated at a nearby loch that still bears their name. Working in tandem with surrounding stone circles, Callanish reflects orderly cycles taking place in the sky and establishes a mediating rhythm with the laws of nature on the land. No wonder a sizeable society was once supported here, drawing from the circles the required energy and know-how with which to live a life in equilibrium. Given such platitudes it is hardly surprising that Callanish should carry a third name, Kallaöarnes, and it too remains remarkably close to its Armenian root: *kal-ogh-anyerz*, 'come to the circle without boundary'; or *kal-ogh-andes*, 'come to the ring of the unseen'.

Linguistically the syllable *kal* is interchangeable with *kar* (stone), so in this context the site invites us 'to attend the stone ring of the unseen'. Either option aptly describes a location from where one crosses an invisible frontier into the Otherworld.

Trying to solve the remote past is like a forensic dissection of a dustbin, rummaging through flotsam and jetsam to piece together a reasonable argument that might explain a given event. Does the answer represent the truth? Probably not. Only those originally involved with the event know the absolute truth. But the more dustbins one dissects the more evidence procured, the closer one comes to the truth. In this spirit I wish to push the envelope on the matter of Kallaöarnes.

In the name Kallaöarnes we find an overlap of Celtic and Sumerian languages with Armenian as the common root. *Kalle* typically refers to a harbor or landing place, and indeed the remains of a jetty exists at the foot of the Callanish ridge where pilgrims arrived from as far away as the Mediterranean. Öarnes, or possibly Oannes, is a Greek transliteration of the Mesopotamian sage Ou-anna, or Ur-annu depending on the dialect, who is portrayed in stone reliefs as half-man, half-fish, indicating the seafaring origin of this traveling god. The name is a contraction of Uanadapa, *adapa* meaning 'wise', the root of 'adept'. The point to this is that such adepts are identified around the world by a basket they carry. Still known throughout Polynesia and New Zealand as a *kete*, the basket symbolically holds the sum of a tribe's sacred knowledge, so any individual associated with this icon holds a very high office within tribal temple culture. Was Kallaöarnes named in tribute to this

Vetehinen.

sage? Yes and no. The name is actually a title held by any number of figures, thus the third name for Callanish informs us this was a port where wisdom keepers alighted to attend to their sacred dealings, as reflected in another variation of Tursachan, the Armenian phrase *tur'sagar*, effectively the 'gateway of the basket', thus reflecting the stone circle's status as a repository of sacred knowledge.

Ur-annu holds a kete.

Callanish was not the only place where these sages were present. In the folklore of Orkney, the miniscule island of Eynhallow was regarded as a particularly holy domain, originally the summer residence of the Finnfolk, a group of shape-shifting sorcerers known as *mer-people*, who rowed from Norway with just seven strokes of the oar on a ship they rendered invisible. Described as half human, half fish, very tall and handsome, they could take on full human form whenever they wished but preferred to avoid direct contact with humans whenever possible. A visitor from Mesopotamia would draw a direct parallel with Enki, the Anunaki god, who was also known by Armenians as Haya and Hayk. Later he becomes known as Ur-anu. The long-bearded, fish-tailed Enki led a group of seven Apkallu and similarly made human contact only if and when a situation absolutely demanded it. As people migrated north-westward from Sumer, this water god entered Finnish mythology and became

A mer person.

vetehinen, a powerful, bearded healer and magician still depicted with a fish tail. After the account reached Scandinavia it was a brief sea voyage across to Orkney and Lewis.

Like Enki and his sages, the Finnfolk were said to spend the winter in an underwater abode that was also their ancestral home. The given name of this location was Hildaland, literally 'hidden land', an island made invisible by fog. Since the story and the characters in the original Mesopotamian account describe events which took place during the great flood 11,700 years ago, the myth describes a time of rising seas that saw the islands of the gods disappear, which explains why their lands are repeatedly described as invisible or under the ocean.[27]

Predictably, invading Catholic priests transformed the magical Finnfolk into stern, gruesome brutes who raided the islands to prey upon ordinary citizens and steal women for wives. The cure? Tell the peasants to paint a Christian cross on the bottom of their hulls for protection and never shall they be afflicted by Finnfolk.

Enki.

A few minutes on a motorboat from Eynhallow – although having experienced the area on what locals described as "a calm day," I wouldn't recommend it – is the hamlet of Evie, where we find a prehistoric settlement. The name may be a corruption of Ea-vie, a term in Basque language meaning 'Ea lives', Ea being the god Enki. Since a substantial part of Basque originates in Armenia, we find its root *E'Ar* to mean 'the god exists'.[28]

The prevalence of Armenian language is similarly observed in the naming of islands in the Inner Hebrides. At first glance the long island of Jura might owe its name to *jur*, the Armenian word for water, but just because two names are similar doesn't mean they are related. In the 7th century, Jura became the seat of power of the Gaelic Dál Riata kings. One wonders what they might have thought of their abode having taken its name from *jurøy*, the old Norse term for 'the island of udders', based on the honest observation of its prominent conical mountains, the Paps of Jura, as upturned mammary glands. However, the earlier Armenian root word *diruhi* is based on exactly the same observation but put more delicately as 'lady', thus making Jura the 'island of the lady'.

Another notable Hebridean island is Arran, or more accurately in Scots Gaelic, Arainn. Its namesake, the ancient city Ar-han, is located between the Kura and Ara rivers in the Armenian Highlands. Meaning 'Place of the Worshippers of Ar', it is dated to c.7500 BC and once featured monumental buildings. The word *Ara-inn* itself is Armenian for 'nine gods', in reference to the antediluvian deities and founders of the region, so it may be for this very reason that Arran the island boasts such a high concentration of stone circles, standing stones, and giants graves (over 1000 according to a recent survey) for such a relatively small land.[29] Not to forget the plethora of horned mounds resembling those of Sardinia.[30] The variant *Ariun* means 'blood relationship', a fitting word for a meeting place of mortals claiming descent from gods.

Paps of Jura.

Similar holy status was bestowed upon another island, Iona, favored by a disproportionate number of kings and queens as their final place of rest, and as a place for spiritual introspection by the Culdee, those hermits in white tunics, named for an Armenian god,[31] who migrated all the way from the warm, sunny Near East to live in seclusion on a wet, cold and windy rock. Like so many places in Scotland settled by different people over many epochs, multiple names have been given to this holy island, but the four oldest sources at least agree on Hy, along with the variants Hii, Eu and Eoa.[32]

As mentioned earlier, *Hy* is a contraction of *Hayk*, referring to Orion as well as a person of Armenian origin. On this foundation we construct the compound word *Hy-ogh-na*, 'the ring of Orion', or in its pure literal form 'the ring of people associated with Orion'. A ring in its metaphoric sense refers to a council of people. In its literal sense, it may refer to the two major circles of stones that once existed on the island, whose memory was recorded by early travelers. As such it presents Iona as a place of council, and the memory of what was conducted there under sacred office was engrained in the land long enough to compel high-ranking individuals in future days to be associated with the status such holy ground confers, long after the wisdom keepers who originally settled here had departed this earthly domain.

The memory of words, it seems, offers useful clues to Scotland's ancient architects and the inspiration behind the monuments they left behind. All that remains is to learn about their origins, and for that we must journey east to the Armenian Highlands.

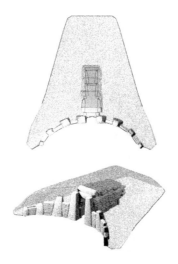

Carn Ban horned mound. Arran.

Beehive and teepee houses on Jura in 1850,
with the paps in the distance.

A stone at Karahunj. Or maybe Brodgar or Callanish?

ARMENIAN CRADLE

t is a sad testimony to the human condition that even as late as the 20th century there have been concerted efforts to erase Armenia from world history and collective memory, most notably by Turkish and Azerbaijani authorities. Taking revisionism to a ludicrous degree, upon the closing of the First World War, the Turkish government obliterated the name *Armenia* from maps just to cover up its genocide, while neighboring Azerbaijan, founded as recently as 1918, appropriated Armenia's 4000-year old statehood. [1] Armenians were redefined as newcomers, moved to the region in 1828 by Russian tsars no less, in an effort to legitimize the hijacking of Armenian territory, history and culture.

This alone inspired me to look into the country's history, and since its language is all over Scotland, doing so might just explain how people from one of the oldest civilizations on Earth could have ended up 3000 miles from their point of origin. Little did I know that I was about to wander into one of the most complicated and brain-twisting histories of any people ever to exist.

When Akkadian ruler Naram-Sin defeated King Ris-Adad-Tesub to conquer Armanum in 2250 BC, he gave the world a glimpse of a people possessing self-determined military strength that up to that point had made them virtually unconquerable. "Never since the creation of mankind has any king among kings taken Armani,"[2] he boasted.

With the exception of Sumerian epic poems and more boastful claims by Babylonian and Hittite kings of their invasions, everything about Armenia and its people remained obscure outside the region until the rise of the kingdom of Urartu in the 9th century BC. To compound the issue, the name Urartu itself was mispronounced by western academics; in reality it is a corruption of Arrarra, the name of Armenia's sacred mountain and epicentre of its history.[3] In support of this hypothesis, regional histories refer to Armina/Armeni as Urastu/Urartu, thus Urartians and Araratians and Armenians were one and the same people, worshipping the same god, Haldi, a linguistic variant of the Armenian sky god Hayk.[4]

Yet this simplified overview has deeper roots. Ancient Armenia was once known by the double name Armennia-Hayastan, symbolizing the divine marriage between the Sun god Ar and the Earth goddess Haya.[5] Variations of the name include Armani, Armanu, and Armanim, along with the contracted Arman, and Arime, which back in the day was a large swathe of territory incorporating upper Mesopotamia, specifically its mountainous northern region. The names all mean the same thing, 'Land of the Sons of the God Ar'.[6]

I was about to congratulate myself on making sense of this historical entanglement until I came across yet another layer of the story. Around 3000 BC the region of Armenia was also referred to as Subartu as well as Mitanni – two states rarely unified, often divided

into autonomous regions, whose names were used as geographic terms covering a large linguistic and cultural community that included Sumeria and Akkadia as well as the entire Armenian Highlands.[7] And yet the royal capital city of Subartu was itself named Armany.[8] Indeed, Armenians and Subari may have been one and the same people, as both shared long-established traditions of industry, metallurgy, cultural integrity, and a high degree of architectural skill, all of which spread south to establish the anomalous and sudden civilization we've come to know as Sumer.[9]

There are indications that the native people of the Armenian Highlands were also the earliest settlers of Southern Mesopotamia. As the people of Subur, they were already migrating to Sumer by 4500 BC, where their archaeological stratum is overlaid by the later

Sumerian culture. At least two hundred parallels exist between Subarian-Armenian and Sumerian languages, from which it can be deduced that an advanced culture was already extant throughout the Armenian region and neighboring Asia Minor and Anatolia prior to 4500 BC.[10] It is also postulated that the Suburi were already residing in the pre-Sumerian city of Eridu, especially as its earliest name was HA.A-S-ba-ri, a linguistic variant of the name of its inhabitants.[11]

Then around 3000 BC something changed. Armenians rallied as a single entity around their legendary forefather Hayk (borrowing his honorary name from the tutelary god), and from this point forward these Indo-European people[12] became collectively known as Armenians.

These 'People of the God Ar/Ara'[13] are ancient beyond description. Coming under the tutelage of Hayk the god, they referred to themselves as Hay-armens, 'people of Orion', a concept best illustrated by the Arabic phrase *hayy*, 'life', as in the breath that is found in all nature and throughout the universe.[14]

To round up this complex yet fascinating history, bear in mind that Hayk refers to a person, a people *and* a constellation. The name is expressed in Indian sacred literature as Hayu, Ayu, and Anu,[15] and this will be of great significance as we progress.

Long before I learned all the above, I had felt an irrational impulse to travel to Armenia, and since I prefer to perform my research *in situ*, no sooner did I entertain the idea of a visit than Armenian nationals began befriending me, as though my intentions were magnetically transmitted into the collective subconscious and reached people suitably placed to assist my research. It's times like these that I really love what I do for a living. I was just about to extend my stay in Egypt and book a flight to Yerevan, the capital, when war erupted between Turkish-supported Azerbaijan and Armenia over an on-going territorial dispute dating back to 1918. My plan had to be shelved for the time being, proving that the gods have limited control over our earthly affairs.

With many etymological and genetic clues linking Scotland and Sardinia to this region, I wanted to get into the prehistory of Armenia to find other tangible connections. I was to discover, however, that given its challenging and sometimes impenetrable terrain, not to mention the volatility of regional politics, archaeological activity in modern-day Armenia has been scarce. The majority of documentation lies buried – literally and politically – and the greater part of the most important region, Western Armenia, remains closed to research. Naturally this only raised my curiosity further.

Although most literature on local prehistory is absent for the time being, given how the people were the progenitors of Sumerian civilization, it is not surprising that Sumerian epic literature presents this land they called Aratta as the cradle of gods, immortals and divine laws, already established beyond doubt by the time a flood engulfed the globe in 9703 BC.[16] There is little doubt that the earliest inhabitants were ahead of the game with regard to understanding how the universe works. A petroglyph estimated to be around 7000 years old was found carved on a boulder near Lake Sevan, showing the Earth as a ball with four humanoids standing at each quarter, two of them upside down in the lower hemisphere.[17]

It is recorded that Aratta was a substantial city in the Ararat Plain by

189

4000 BC, located on a volcanic cone near the source of the Metsamor river, surrounded by water on every side by means of natural and artificial moats, in essence terraforming a pregnant belly – from which the river receives its name, 'Great Mother'. Aratta was further protected by a monumental round tower and a cyclopean turreted wall, outside of which were built residences on vast elevations. Artefacts prove the site was already at a very developed stage, with ritual temples and ziggurats posted on adjacent hills, and astronomical sites used to observe, among other objects, the rising of Sirius. A major shrine called Karmir-K'arer (Red Stones) once stood in the northwest of the city, along with burial or ritual chambers constructed with huge monoliths. A smelting industry, animal husbandry and viniculture also attest to what was undoubtedly an early urban revolution.[18]

Prehistoric Armenia also boasted the holy city of Ani, located east of Kars. It may owe its name from a temple presided by the mother goddess Anahit, meaning 'golden-haired', one of the earliest records of a being who we today would assume to be Scandinavian. Ani was also one of the ancient world's largest cities, at one point its architecture was the most technically and artistically advanced of its kind. It must have carried considerable spiritual and cultural weight because the city became the focal point of a disproportionate number of religious buildings, even into historic times, before they were razed by incoming Christian forces who subsequently built their churches upon the megalithic foundations of earlier temples.[19]

What might these ancient architects have looked like? Our blonde goddess aside, Akkadian inscriptions describe Subarian people as red- or fair-skinned, of light complexion, with women much valued for their "fair and pleasant appearance." Red hair also differentiated Subarians from the black-haired Sumerians,[20] and the

190

early inhabitants of Asia Minor were disproportionally long-headed (dolichocephalic).[21] It would seem that, just as in Sardinia, and to a lesser extent the Scottish isles, there were two distinct races living side-by-side in the Armenian Highlands.

As to the megalithic culture they generated, as might be expected in a region that hosted the most ancient of cultures and witnessed endless conflicts that came looking for them, much of Armenian prehistory is recumbent. Just as the megaliths of Scotland were recovered from the peat, so the stones of Armenia are slowly being rediscovered by agriculture, by accident or by curious individuals relying on tidbits handed down through folk memory. Many monuments remain buried in deep sediment, toppled by the seismic activity afflicting the region, but for the most part felled by invading people with opposing views, or by the incursion of Christianity that razed everything in its path and then built its own pantheons with the stones of the very monuments it destroyed. Then, for good measure, they burned just about every Armenian book available, a

Vishap.

191

crime against humanity it would repeat hundreds of years later in Central America.

Still, the region on the south and west shores of Lake Sevan has a respectful cache of standing stones, petroglyphs and rock observatories perched on the ancient mounds of Vardenis, Metsamor and Syunic.[22] In 1880 the writer Atrpet rediscovered unusual stones called *vishaps*, literally 'serpent stones', enormous cigar-shaped menhirs carved from a single block often in the form of a snake or fish, the tallest being around 17 feet. Two decades later, palaeontologists excavating in the region of Garni collected stories from residents about *vishaps* deliberately buried or destroyed in the Gegham mountains, leading to a resurgence of interest in these unusual monoliths.[23]

Prior to 3000 BC *vishaps* were installed in underground water sources, or above ground near sacred springs, but there's more to this simple association. While it is true that local mythologies link the stones with water deities or spirits, new evidence shows they were also used as central pillars surrounded by mounds called 'tombs of the giants', despite no site as yet showing signs of the mounds having been used for burial.[24] Radiocarbon dating of charcoal in a pit inside one chamber shows human activity in 5215 BC. Archaeologists also discovered that the original standing stones were sometimes deliberately felled and encompassed within later mounds, suggesting a continuation of veneration long after the original site had served its purpose.[25] I couldn't help but recall Maeshowe and the way it appears to have been built around an earlier group of standing stones. What is also interesting is the design and method of construction of the Armenian mounds, how they are reminiscent of those on Orkney, and even more so, those on the Scottish mainland at Kilmartin.

Some years ago I came across a series of unnerving images of a monument perched dramatically on the edge of a mountain ridge to the south of Lake Sevan. I say unnerving because I was only too familiar with the general design, just not in Armenia. Named Karahunj, it consists of over 233 standing stones arranged in four avenues leading to a central oval-shaped stone circle. Seen from above it is like looking at an older displaced cousin of Callanish.

The name Karahunj breaks down into *kar* (stone) and *hunj* (sound), thus it is the 'Place of the Sounding Stones'. Its linguistic counterpart in England is Stonehenge, whose original bluestones possess a sonic quality when struck, as reflected in the name of their origin in Wales, Maenclochog, the 'Place of the Ringing Rocks'.

One other fact binds Stonehenge, Callanish and Karahunj: each of their folklore assigns the building of these three Neolithic sites to a race of giants.

For a while I thought I was the only person who'd made the connection between Callanish and Karahunj until I came across the work of the late Paris Herouni, an Armenian genius whose *résumé* runs to three pages, together with 350 published scientific papers. He also holds 23 patents. Despite a formidable life in the scientific arena, however, one can tell that his passion lay in Karahunj, where he invested years of study, focusing specifically on its archaeoastronomical alignments.

Herouni was quite taken by the eighty stones featuring carved conical sight holes, 2.7 by 1.9-inch in diameter, all of which can be used to calculate the mid-heaven elevation of specific stars, the determining of the axis of rotation of the Earth, and computation of the planet's

precession.[26] Stone 63 is particularly worthy of note because it is used to determine the latitude of the site itself.[27]

A magnetometer survey of the site found a distribution of telluric currents feeding into the central circle, just as they do in its counterparts around the world.[28]

After years of calculations, Herouni and his team reasoned that Karahunj may have begun operating as early as the spring equinox in 22,946 BC,[29] which is not far-fetched considering the eroded condition of the stones. There is also the fact that in order to calculate the Precessional Cycle (the slow-motion rotation of the Earth's axis) one must first be aware that the phenomenon exists, which requires a person to stand on the same spot patiently observing the same object move across the sky until its return to the same position 25,920 years later – what Greek astronomers referred to as The Great Year. But Herouni also noted that the site had been refined by 5500 BC, to the degree that rising and setting azimuths of

no less than nine bright stars were being calculated at this specific time.[30] Many of these are relevant to our quest because five of them were principal stars in Orion. Two hundred years later the astronomer priests of Orkney were making the same observation, as though operating with a similar intent.

Just as in the Scottish islands, according to folklore, Karahunj was a place for astronomical calculation as well as an academy of learning. Since the stones themselves held the information, the site's name reflected its function as a place where the rocks 'spoke' or 'sang'. All this earth magic took place under the patronage of the Sun god Ar, and Tir, patron god of science, written language and the arts – two names comparable to the Egyptian gods åa-Ra[31] and Twt (transliterated by the Greeks as Thoth).

Just as overlaps exist between Armenian and Egyptian loan words in Scotland, so another exists between Egyptian and Armenian temple cultures. One of the oldest continuously operating astronomical academies was stationed in Harranu, a town in what used to be upper Mesopotamia where human activity has been present since at least 8000 BC.[32] Harranu generally translates as 'valley of Anu', and it was once a location where the Shining Ones, the white tunic-wearing Watchers, were said to have resided.[33] These keen observers of the stars

Shapes of Karahunj megaliths also found in Scotland.

were known by the Egyptians as *Sba*, literally 'star people', later to be known as Sabeans,[34] but whether the *Sba* and the Shining Ones were one and the same people is not clear. However, the fact is that every year the *Sba* would undertake a pilgrimage to the Giza Plateau to expand their studies, and were still doing so in 1900 BC, according to the commemorative *stelae* these astronomer priests left when they lived beside the Sphinx.[35] Perhaps it comes as no surprise that Egyptian and Armenian/Mesopotamian cultures observed the motion of the heavens using the cycles of Sirius, Sun and Moon. What is surprising, though, is that the enigmatic Egyptian unit of measure, the Cubit, which, very practically, was taken to be the length of the pharaoh's arm to his elbow, finds its counterpart in the ancient Armenian *armung*, a unit of measure meaning 'elbow'. If this cultural interaction is indeed as ancient as it appears, then the extreme date proposed by Herouni for Karahunj may not seem so radical, after all, the

A Sabean priest.

Egyptian King List specified on the Turin Papyrus lists the first ruler ascending the throne around 39,000 BC.

I've spent ample time familiarizing myself with the stone circles in Orkney and Lewis to recognize their unique artistic qualities. In ancient times there was an art to selecting stones whose natural shape expressed the purpose for which they were intended. That's quite a laborious exercise in itself, especially so if the intent requires a monolith in the shape of an isosceles triangle – not exactly something nature creates haphazardly, if at all. Common sense therefore suggests the stone circles utilize a combination of natural megaliths and others shaped by human hand. What I was not prepared to find was the same unusual shapes – trapezoids, right-angle shelves, isosceles triangles, spermia and teardrops – duplicated in Brodgar, Callanish, and now Karahunj. If my observation is correct, it means that the shapes of stones form a common language used to perform functions that recur at different sites. For example, a stone with a right-angle shelf might mark the rising of the Moon, a trapezoid might mark Orion, and so forth.

I thought the overlaps between Karahunj and Callanish were impressive in themselves until I learned of a remote Neolithic megalithic site called Mawkyrwat, located in the Khasi Hills of northern India. Armenian history states that migration to what became Sumeria also spread east through the Arya and Ayu tribes,[36] who settled in northern India by 3000 BC and undoubtedly took their root traditions there.[37] The site in question consists of a massive stone circle, much like Brodgar but consisting of some 90 stones, with a raised platform in the center where a group of taller stones, around 19 feet in height, forms an arc. If a resident of Lewis, or Stenness for that matter, was shown a photograph of this place they

Mawkyrwat.

would think it had been taken in Scotland, because the shapes of the stones are dead-ringers for those on Orkney and Lewis, right down to the height. The ethnologist Christoph Von Fürer-Haimendorf probably said it best when he wrote of the site: "There is no race in the Asiatic mainland which had developed megalithic technique to such a degree...their row of huge menhirs...are among the most impressive megalithic monuments."[38]

Territorially speaking, this opens up the question of how much influence might the astronomer-architects of the Armenian Highlands have had beyond Sardinia, the

Khasi Hill monuments in 1876, with central stone identical to Callanish.

Mediterranean and Scotland. While such an inquiry is well beyond the perimeter of this book, I do wish to use one example to highlight the possibility of this academy of savants having once been part of a global enterprise, a hypothesis I covered extensively in my previous work, *The Missing Lands*. The elements that make Karahunj what it is are found in another distant sacred site, similarly perched on a dramatic hilltop and surrounded by a range of hills that form an inter-cardinal view of the sky. Protected by a monolith carved with the image of a tutelary goddess, the landscape temple in question, on the south island of New Zealand, is called Kura Tawhiti, a Maori name meaning 'distant school'. Along with two attendant sites, the location is collectively known as 'the Crucible'.[39] Up until now I took the phrase at face value, until I discovered the word *kura* in Armenian also means 'crucible'. The rest of the word breaks down accordingly: Ta is an Egyptian and Polynesian definitive, as in 'the' or 'belonging to', and *hiti* is an alternative spelling of *Hati*, a variant name of the fertility goddess Heba.[40] Thus to an Armenian sailing to New Zealand, *Kura Ta Hati* means 'crucible of the goddess'. And as its Maori name clearly implies, Kura Tawhiti, like Karahunj, was an ancient academy.

The traditions of the prehistoric settlers of New Zealand, the Waitaha, record the tribe's interactions with the original builders, right down to an accurate physical description, and thanks to this Kura Tawhiti, Karahunj and the megalithic sites of Orkney and Lewis are bound

Orion alignment above the calendar stone.

together. These gods of New Zealand were real people who possessed a thorough understanding of the stars. They were also renowned long distance seafarers with ties to Egypt, Mesopotamia, Easter Island and South America.[41] Called Uru-kehu, they are described as tall, light-skinned, red- or blonde-haired, and uniquely associated with Orion, particularly its belt stars, each of which are represented to this day by three *kete* (baskets), into which the three families of Waitaha wisdom keepers have been pouring the knowledge provided by the Uru-kehu for over 11,000 years.[42] That's an impressive tribal tradition, to say the least.

And since old habits die hard, there exists a Calendar Stone at Kura Tawhiti that memorializes the first appearance of Orion's Belt above it on the winter solstice of 12,400 BC, with the entire constellation following suit in 10,400 BC.[43]

Personally I find these associations provocative and invigorating, least of all because they challenge our preconception of how ancient cultures have hitherto been portrayed as rudimentary. Such revelations paint a picture of people for whom there existed few physical boundaries as they spread their knowledge far and wide, expanding our own cultural horizon in the process.

I dwell on this on August 11 just as people gather at Karahunj to celebrate the pre-Christian New Year, to watch the rising of Orion above this ancient masterpiece on the Armenian plateau.

Calendar stone with Kura Tawhiti in the distance.

*Before its excavation in the 19th century
the Kurgan of Kerch was believed to
have been a natural hill.*

TRAVELING LORDS

ritten by order of Alfred the Great in the 9th century, the *Anglo-Saxon Chronicle* makes it very clear where the first Britons came from: "The island Britain is 800 miles long, and 200 miles broad. And there are in the island five nations: English, Welsh (or British), Scottish, Pictish, and Latin. The first inhabitants were the Britons, who came from Armenia, and first peopled Britain southward."[1]

There was some debate as to whether the writer may have made an unconscious error by mistaking Armenia for Armorica, the earlier name for Brittany, because the account appears to follow a similar work compiled two hundred years earlier by the Venerable Bede, in which the Benedictine monk clearly refers to the French province.[2] Since the *Anglo-Saxon Chronicle* specifically describes the migration as "southward", i.e. from Scotland, and Armorica lies *south* of Britain, the answer is self evident. Nevertheless, there is truth to both accounts.

It is estimated that the first Armenian expeditions into Europe took place sometime around the sixth millennium BC, locating new settlements, and building monuments and observatories with similar purposes to Karahunj.[3] This coincides with the period memorialized by the temples on Orkney. Wherever they traveled, place names followed, leaving behind a linguistic fingerprint. When they settled along the north-western coast of France, they gave the region a name. To quote Paris Herouni: "For Armenians the concept of Mother was so high that even the Sun after each day in sunset went to rest with his Mother, i.e. beyond Armenian mountains or into the sea. From there came also the word Armorika, the old Armenian name of the Brittany Peninsula, where lived Bretons and Celts: Armenians. Armorika in Armenian means 'The Sun Goes To Mother', because all people saw every day that the Sun sets into the Atlantic Ocean."[4]

Brittany is home to one of the largest concentrations of megalithic sites in the world. A survey at the end of the 19th century by the French government listed over 80,000 dolmens, menhirs and passage mounds, yet this impressive statistic only represented the mere fraction of monuments that survived a devastating rise in sea level during the fourth millennium BC,[5] leaving the remainder to systematically face the wrath of the Church. The epicenter of this megalithic culture, the old Breton town Kargneagh (Carnac) derives its name from the Armenian *kar-nakh*, 'the principal stones', while the regional city Vannes is named for Lake Van in Armenia.[6]

Conversely, Er Grah, a collection of ceremonial chambers, passage mounds,

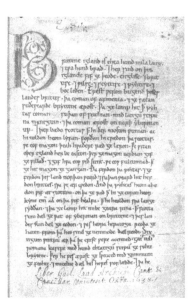

Anglo-Saxon Chronicle.

and the tallest menhir ever erected, is rooted in the Egyptian *åar-gåh*, 'chapel of ascent'.[7]

From Britanny it was a short voyage across the English Channel to Wales, or as it was originally called, Cymru (pronounced *kumri*), named for Armenia's ancient father city Kumayri, which still exists today.[8] The historian Martiros Kavoukjian notes how the roots of the Cymru people lie with the Cimmerians of the ancient Armenian Highlands, who were known locally as Gamirk.[9] Their original migration route took them north to the Ukrainian steppes and the Black Sea, and from there to northern Britain. They arrived there with two notable cultural accoutrements of their homeland: the first, woven twill garments with geometric patterns that became the iconic Scottish kilt. Fragments of fabric taken from the Siberian steppes and dated to 4500 BC reveal they were made from sheep with woollen coats suitable for spinning such yarn, five hundred years before they were introduced into Europe.

Their second cultural contribution to Scotland? That most euphonious of musical instruments, the bagpipe.

Their progeny subsequently left a linguistic trail throughout England. An analysis of English language shows 55% of its words are of Celt-Armenian origin.[10] Two notable examples are the fertility god Damuzid, whose name was given to the river running through London, the Thames, and the name by which the island as a whole was known, *Bh-ar-at-An*, the 'Place of the kind Sun worshippers of An' – *An* being a linguistic variation of the god *Ar*. We know this land today as Britannia.[11]

It seems Alfred the Great did us a huge favor by commissioning the *Anglo-Saxon Chronicle*, as it opened up a whole new area of investigation. As to the Angles, those Germanic people originate from a region in Armenia where once existed a fortress called Anggh Tun, 'Angel town', named after the god Angegh, from which arises the word 'angel'. [12]

We now have a general picture of the people who migrated from the regions bordering the Black Sea to Europe and eventually found themselves in the Scottish Isles around 5500 BC. Their linguistic, genetic and architectural fingerprints are evidence of this, but in order to pinpoint who the ancient architects dwelling among them might have been, it is necessary to travel 12,000 years back into the prehistory of upper Mesopotamia and the Armenian Highlands.

In previous chapters I touched upon the foundation of Ar-me-ni, 'land of the sons of Ar', god of rejuvenation and the sky (and sometimes goddess, this entity was most likely androgynous). I also pointed out in torturous detail how language and pronunciation evolves with migration and topography. The pain of this exercise will now bear fruit.

Throughout the Armenian Highlands and its immediate regions, the name *Ar* or *Ara* is interchangeable with *Aru*, *Anu*, *Ani*, and *Ana*,[13] with the latter co-opted as Ann, the mother of the gods in the Celtic pantheon. Of all these variations it is Anu who is perhaps the most familiar.

In my previous book *The Missing Lands* I dwelt upon the people of Anu in great detail, so to save repeating myself I will simply conduct an overview. Around 12,000 years ago a civilization of god-like people lived alongside yet separate from other humans. They were known by different names around the world: Hayhayuapanti in South America, Kaanul in Yucatan, Offiusa in Iberia,

Lóng in China, Aku Shemsu Hor in Egypt, Uru-kehu in New Zealand and Polynesia, Naga in Indo-China, Anunaga in India, and finally, Anu-naki in Mesopotamia and the regions around the Caspian and Black seas.[14] Regardless of territory, title or name, the Anu-naki are unanimously described as very tall, light-skinned, red-haired and green-eyed, or blonde and blue-eyed. Ancient compilers such as Pliny the Elder, Hippocrates, Josephus, Herodotus, Amianes Marcealis, even the Han Chinese general Han Xin, referred to them as Scythians or Suevi.

Relative to our quest, they were also described by every ancient culture with whom they interacted as master seafarers and astronomers, not to mention architects of extraordinary monuments in stone, all the attributes required in the people we've been searching for in connection with Scotland's sacred places.

Anu-naki is best translated as 'people of the sky god Anu', and their prime settlement was said to be near the Caspian Sea,[15] the region generally known as the Armenian Highlands. Governance was undertaken by the Lords of Anu, a deiform family consisting of seven males and one female. Their Grand Assembly once sat in the prehistoric city of Nippur, where each of the eight lords held a ring of divine justice; they in turn were governed by Anu, who

Aku Shemsu Hor at Edfu.

held the one ring that bound them all. This group of god-kings and queens was described as the original rulers who were "lowered from heaven," progenitors of a divine bloodline. This assembly became the template for the nine kingdoms presided by the god Odin in the Scandinavian *Völsunga Saga*.[16] Their bloodline was bestowed with the nickname People of the Serpent, from which arose the houses of the Naga priests of India, the Kaanul dynasty of the Maya, and the Dragon Kings of the East. The name serves two functions: first, it describes their ability to understand and harness the telluric forces of the Earth, which in virtually every culture are represented by serpents or dragons. And second, the governing lords in Mesopotamia and Egypt were anointed with *mus-hus*, the fat from a monitor lizard, a word that gave rise to the Hebrew *meschiachs*, 'the anointed ones', while their Welsh counterparts bore the title Pendragon, 'Head Dragon'. Since this anointment gave the skin a lustrous sheen, the Anu were awarded the title Shining Ones, which simultaneously defined the luminous demeanor of a people exuding superior knowledge.[17] The Shining Ones also formed the root stock of the Egyptian divine bloodline, the Aku Shemsu Hor, literally 'Shining Ones, Followers of Horus', who governed for 13,420 years until the first pharaoh of "purely human bloodline" ascended the throne of Egypt in 3113 BC,[18] meaning that their lineage was in existence for over 18,000 years.[19]

Naga princess.

According to Indo-European religious belief, the

shining light of the sky was regarded as the ultimate abode of a supreme creative force, a father/mother god. The supernatural and the physical were not regarded as separate but as interconnected and interdependent, the actions and effects of one affecting the other and vice versa. To tamper with this universal tenet is to invite self-destruction. The laws of nature can be manipulated within the boundaries of the laws themselves – consequently what we define as magic was nothing more than the understanding and application of these laws. Any person with a grasp of these principles acquired significant status as a priest or sage whereupon they were awarded the title Shining One. By 4000 BC this royal pedigree came to be defined by the prefix *el*, the Mesopotamian term for 'shining', developing in Babylon as *ellu* when referring specifically to 'a Shining One'. The title then arrives in Wales as *ellyn*, in Ireland as *aillil*, and in England as *elf*.[20] In the Gaelic county of Cornwall, in south-western England, the word *el* was the equivalent of the Anglo-Saxon *engel* and the old French *angele* which became the English *angel*.[21]

This offers us additional clarification as to the origin of the 'shining one' who was said to have walked the avenue of stones at Callanish, a connection made all the more tangible by the descriptions of such priests wearing white tunics, much like the garments worn by the Lords of Anu and their accompanying magician-priests, the Watchers, who, it should be pointed out, were all associated with Orion.[22]

This also answers the riddle of the Bay of Angels, the anomalous name given to the waterway adjacent to the stone circles of Orkney where white robed priests known as Papae once formed a secular group, as well as that of the Hill of Angels, the sacred mound on Iona, similarly attended by white-robed individuals.

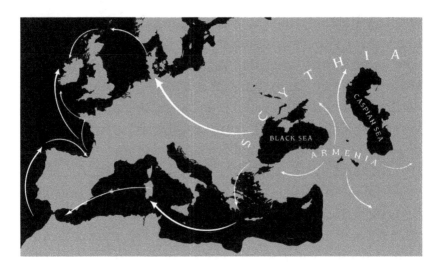

A parallel school of thought believes these sages were none other than the Druidhe, a valid point since this priesthood was present throughout the Scottish Isles. Yet the Druidhe didn't appear casually out of nowhere with a fully developed curriculum. As their title, the Lords of Light, suggests, they were the continuation of an age-old tradition dating back into prehistory, since the same aphorism applied to the Anu-naki.

There's a second part to the Armenian migration to Britain and it too is referenced in the *Anglo-Saxon Chronicle*: "Then happened it, that the Picts came south from Scythia, with long ships, not many; and, landing first in the northern part of Ireland, they told the Scots that they must dwell there." Long before these people became Picts they were known as Scythians, a fact known by the Scots when they wrote of their Scythian origins in *The Declaration of Arbroath* of 1320: "We know, and from the chronicles and books of the ancients, we and that among other famous nations our own, the Scots, has been graced with widespread renown. It journeyed from Greater Scythia by way of the Tyrrhenian Sea [Sardinia] and the Pillars of Hercules, and dwelt for a long course of time in Spain among the most savage people."

Emperor Justinius II once described the Scythians as "among the most ancient races in the world, older than the Egyptians." That's quite a claim given that the reign of pharaohs listed in the *Turin Papyrus* begins around 39,000 BC, and yet, according to the historian Pliny, the Scythians themselves were preceded by people from the Armenian Highlands, "the Aramei."[23] By 5500 BC the two were indistinguishable,[24] to the point where the king of Scythia, Paruyr Skayorti, was himself of Armenian descent.[25] This amalgamation of cultures became the foundation of Sumerian civilization, given that Armenian culture as well as Scythian writing precedes Sumerian culture and cuneiform by over one thousand years.[26]

Around 4000 BC the Lords of Anu were still involved in the municipal governance and kingly practices of Sumer (whose name may a derivation of *sumaire*, 'coiled serpent',[27] a nickname of the Lords) while their descendants were also princes of the House of Scythia,[28] described as a noble race by the name Tuadhe d'Anu and identified by Herodotus as the Royal Scythe.[29] Based on the Sumerian term *danu-na,* meaning 'princely offspring of Anu', they too were referred to as Lords of Light. Under the umbrella of Scythia, their dynastic kingship and culture extended over a wide territory, from Asia Minor and Armenia, north to the Black and Caspian seas, into Ukraine and the Siberian steppes, and westwards along the Danube into the Carpathian Mountains and Transylvanian Alps. At one point their rule extended to the Nile River, as the Greek historian Diodorus Siculus reminds us.

Upon reaching Denmark, Sweden and Norway, the Tuadhe d'Anu left their trademark genealogy throughout the region. The image of the Gallic-British tall, pale-skinned, blonde, blue-eyed warrior or flaxen-haired maiden is of Nordic stock, which itself stems from Caucasian roots from around the Black Sea; the red-haired, green or pale-eyed Gaelic types were of noble Scythian origin. They operated an egalitarian caste system with levels of active function but no hierarchy of individual class distinction, from which evolved the Scottish Clan system.[30] They were also noted for their body armor, constructed from small scale-like plates of bronze which, when tarnished to a greenish hue, gave their warriors the appearance of what the Greek geographer Pausanias described as 'dragons'.[31]

As one travels along the Caucasus towards the Ukrainian steppes and west into Crimea, admiring the open plains and big sky country, the landscape is oddly marked by lone, teardrop-shaped hills, which, on approach, reveal themselves to be cyclopean artificial mounds called *kurgans*. The *kurgans* of this region, including south-eastern Europe, are conservatively dated to around 5000 BC.[32] Featuring elegant passage chambers made of tall orthostats, they are precursors of the passage mounds in Scotland and Ireland.

Kurgan derives from the Armenian word *kura-garq*, 'crucible of the social class'. Its later Sumerian variant *E-Kur* ('mountain house') indicates an assembly of the gods, a designated place on the earth where sky and ground are one, hence *E-Kur-gan,* 'mountain sky house' – the most revered of buildings in ancient Sumer. Their architecture was later interpreted in the ziggurats.

In the region of the Black Sea, *kurgans* served multiple purposes. Excavations of the impressive mound named Sengileevskoe-2 near Strovopol revealed a secret rectangular chamber in which no one was buried. Instead the alleged looters ran off with a decomposed body but left behind valuable gold artefacts of superlative quality, along

Scythian initiation ritual.

with three gold cups containing a black residue, analyzed as a brew consisting of opium impregnated with smoke from cannabis, which would have been burned to create a vapor-bath inside the chamber. The engravings on the cups show detailed and dramatic scenes of animals and humans fighting and dying, along with a bearded elder stabbing a younger man in the spinal cord, a feature identical to Mithraic scenes of the hunter stabbing the bull in the same anatomical location. Such graphic images represent the rite of passage into the Scythian Otherworld, which culminates in the metaphoric sacrifice of the immature younger self. *Kurgans* of this type were accessible only to a select group within the temple culture and used for performing the highest level of initiation.[33]

It has been argued that *kurgan* burials were rare, and only then reserved for special adults who were predominantly, but not necessarily, male.[34] One such example is located east of the Caspian Sea in central Siberia. With a base perimeter of 1500 feet, the *kurgan* of Salbyk is half the size of the Great Pyramid of Giza. It originally began as a simple rectangle of megaliths weighing up to 60 tons each, the tips of the stones angled like those of Stenness. The inner perimeter was then gradually filled to create a pyramid-shaped mound estimated to have been 120 feet tall. Such *kurgans* served as meeting places for the Scythian Lords. The central area consisted of clay as well as continuously built structures, each on top of the last, and as the previous habitations deteriorated and disintegrated they took on the form of mounds. Essentially they gathered on ground occupied by their ancestors, sometimes literally, because some *kurgans* became places of physical

Salbyk kurgan. The scale of stones after excavation (below) suggests the reuse of an older megalithic site.

burial, forerunners of the barrows and giants' graves found throughout Britain, Britanny and Ireland.[35] When the *kurgan* of Salbyk was excavated in 1954, the expedition from Moscow State University found a central vault in the form of a seven foot-high truncated pyramid, in which lay the remains of a 70-year-old man and six other people, two of whom were relatives. The burial is estimated to have taken place c.1400 BC.

Genetic studies of the ancient kurgan culture of the region reveal human specimens carrying the same Y-chromosomal and Mitochondrial DNA haplogroups found in the people who migrated from Armenia to northern Europe and Scandinavia, with further data indicating they were blue or green-eyed, fair-skinned and light-haired people.[36]

There is a variation on the theme and it involves circular buildings. The light complexion and noble demeanor of the Tuadhe d'Anu led to their sobriquet 'the fair people'; in time they came to be known by the contracted term *faeries*.[37] The overlap between faery and royalty developed from the Egyptian *per-âa*, the root of 'pharaoh', which means 'great house'.[38] The social structures of the Tuadhe d'Anu were firmly centred upon designated seats of assembly held in circular halls or towers. By association

these became popularly referred to as Fairy Rings.[39] We see the development of this concept in the *nuraghe* of Sardinia, those circular towers used as designated places of assembly by a close-knit religious class, the *nuirag*, 'the just or rightful, white, shining people'. And of course, Dun Carloway, the 'circular stone dwelling of a family of noble race'. It seems the bards of Lewis were right all along when they ascribed such unusual buildings to a race of tall people, "certain strangers", people from afar.

As time progressed and the Tuadhe d'Anu reached Scotland and Ireland, such places of royal assembly became known as *raths*, meaning 'round or circular'. Perhaps the most important Scottish *rath* is found on Dunadd, a solitary crag rising two hundred feet out of a meadow a few miles south of Kilmartin on the Scottish mainland. The name essentially means 'the *dun* on the Ád', named for the adjacent river that wanders from its source in Loch Sitheanach, the 'Loch of the Fairy Mound'.

Dunadd.

Before the surrounding estuary silted, Dunadd was an island, seat of power of the Dál Riata kings who assembled in a ring court on the summit;[40] the entrance leading to it was sliced out of the cliff and marks the winter solstice. On the summit was placed the Lia Fáil, a kingmaking stone possessing magical power and knowledge that uttered like an oracle beneath the foot of the rightful ruler, hence it was referred to as a *cloch labhrais*, a 'talking stone'. According to various overlapping traditions, this stone was brought to the Mound of Inauguration at Tara in Ireland by descendents of the daughter of pharaoh Smenkhare and her husband Niul, prince of the Royal House of Scythia.[41] It is said to have remained there until the 5th century, when it was moved by Fergus Mór, founder of Scotland, as his kingship established a foothold on the mainland and Dunadd became the new seat of power.[42]

The supernatural qualities of this stone are reminiscent of the description by Alverio Cau of an unusual stone he uncovered along with several giant skeletons in Sardinia: "when someone sits above it, it generates

Although a replica, the footprint still aligns to the summer solstice, as well as with the entrance and the winter solstice.

feelings of wellbeing, the stone loses its hardness and acquires a softness. It is as if powerful positive energy is circulated there." [43] Regardless of whether the stone originated in Scythia or Egypt, the fact is it was taken across the Mediterranean to northern Portugal and Spain, with Sardinia conveniently *en route.*

It is plausible that by its description as a 'talking stone' the Lia Fáil may originally have been one of the 'speaking stones' of Karahunj. Although it may seem counter-intuitive for a priestly culture such as the Tuadhe d'Anu to cannibalise an established sacred site, one could argue that preserving the stone from the destruction that befell sacred places throughout Scythia and Armenia justified its removal, especially as the stone, by its very nature, would have retained the energy

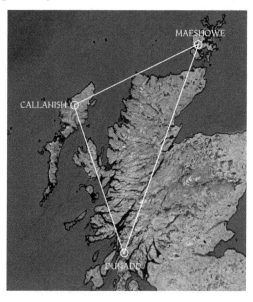

of the site as well as the memory of the land, acting as a talisman and coronation stone, and ensuring the continuation of tradition in a far-off land.

Dunadd was originally spelled Dun At,[44] a linguistic variant of the sky god Ar, thus this circular seat of assembly becomes 'the dwelling of noble race of Ar', which may explain a significant feature on the summit: a footprint carved into the bedrock, where the rightful ruler placed his foot the moment the Sun rose above the horizon on the summer solstice, the peak of solar power, to which said footprint is purposely aligned.

The importance of Dunadd as a point of sacred assembly is further underscored by its location relative to two sites performing similar functions, Callanish and Maeshowe, the three forming a near-perfect right-angle triangle.[45]

The importance of *kurgans* and round towers as the original seats of assembly for the noble Tuadhe d'Anu is perhaps best exemplified by the royal *kurgan* of Kerch in eastern Crimea, a superlative example of ancient architecture. The mound is massive – 60 feet high with a base perimeter over 800 feet. The 120 foot-long entrance passage, built with an acute corbelled vault in the shape of an inverted V, can only be described as regal. It leads to a circular corbelled chamber almost 30 feet high. The mound's original provenance is unknown and during the 1837 excavation nothing was found inside except a crude wooden box. There is nothing here that indicates the chamber was ever intended as a mausoleum: instead it whispers PLACE OF ASSEMBLY for a very special group of people. Anyone who has seen the similarly corbelled interior of Maeshowe cannot help but notice the architectural resemblance between the two, and despite being separated by almost 2000 miles, the buildings share the same general compass direction. While the passage at Maeshowe aligns to the setting of Orion's Belt and the midwinter Sun in 3990 BC, the royal *kurgan* of Kerch observes the exact same alignment down its passageway on the winter solstice of 4600 BC.

With a glorious view out across the Black Sea, ignoring the now semi-industrial hinterland of Kerch around it, you'd might as well be on Orkney looking out across Loch Harray.

Kurgan of Kerch. Looking a lot like Maeshowe.

Ballymeanoch in 1867 and now.

12

THE IRISH CONNECTION

ocated on the Scottish mainland between the islands of Mull, Jura and Arran, the glen of Kilmartin is peppered with passage mounds, stone circles, giants graves, regular graves, stone rows, and an enormous ensemble of rock art – four hundred known sites within a six-mile radius that once made this area a kind of Neolithic metropolis. For a hiker it is a faery wonderland where a topographic map is your best friend and the attentive eye will discover the most magical artefacts of a bygone era hidden among lichen-covered woods.

I love walking here for the peace, but especially for the tangible connection to the ancestors and the environment to which they were umbilically connected. They seem to be but a whisper away at Kintraw, four weathered cairns perched on a dramatic ridge overlooking Loch Craignish, and beyond, the Paps of Jura. The scale of the two principal cairns reflects the size of the Moon relative to the Earth, their axis aligned to the winter solstice sunset.[1] On the southern kerb of the main mound there is a stone box designed as a false door for collecting the light of the Moon at its southern Standstill.[2] But the most enchanting feature of Kintraw is the thin, 13-foot-tall monolith unmistakably depicting the eyes, nose and mouth of a long-headed individual, quite possibly the astronomer priest originally associated with the site.

Down in the meadows beside Kilmartin village, three cairns still look impressive despite the rains having washed away their soil cover, leaving miniature versions of their *kurgan* cousins. According to excavation notes by William Greenwell in 1864, the northern or Glebe Cairn began as a dual-ring stone circle with a long history of ritual before being piled with river stones and reused as graves for an unknown man and woman. The third cairn was specifically a burial site, its internal cist aligned as it is to the pole star, the destination of the soul; carvings of axes and lozenges are near identical to those found in the passage mounds of Carnac. Beside the cist rests a large slab, formerly the lid, carved with over forty cup marks, the sign of a dignitary whose soul was returned to the stars.

The southern, and oldest, cairn forms the end of this linear group of mounds that stretches for three miles.

The Kintraw giant.

Aligned to the northeast, it would have been reserved for ceremonies conducted by wisdom keepers inside its interior chamber composed of schist orthostats, similar in design to those on Orkney. Since it is still accessible after 6000 years via a roof box, each time I bring a group here we perform an undisturbed guided meditation inside the 20-foot chamber that nicely accommodates eight people. I watch them leave very different to when they arrived. Just beyond its perimeter, a small burial cist was added much later in its long history.

Further along the meadow, past inquisitive horses and sheep, two stone circles built c.3500 BC are set within the tranquility of Templewood, the axis pointing to the Major Lunar Standstill moonrise.[3] Once again we see evidence of a site reused for burial, except here it was done with enormous sensitivity. While the central cist is aligned to the pole star, the inner circle of stones around the cist was constructed with a diameter relative to the original circle in a ratio of 4:1, equivalent to the diameter of the Earth relative to the Moon.

A long walk along damp grassy fields, sustained by the munching of an oat cake, leads to the two parallel

Nether Largie ceremonial mound.

stone rows of Ballymeanoch, an elegant collection of tall sandstones once used to record the Lunar Standstill, the winter solstice, and Orion's Belt in 4000 BC. The main row once consisted of seven megaliths, three of which have since been harvested to build field walls; one stone in particular was much beloved of villagers, for it featured a hole similar to the Odin Stone beside Stenness and, like the Odin Stone, suffered a similar fate. Luckily the second impressive megalith still stands with its seventy cup marks, making it the most extensively carved stone in Scotland.

Perhaps my favorite site is Slockavullin because at first the stones don't seem part of a unified working mechanism. A sinuous monolith carved with forty cup-and-ring marks stands at the center like a star map; a set of two inline stones lie a ways to the north, with two more to the south. Together they form a long, narrow X. The Scottish engineer and archaeoastronomer Alexander Thom once described this as "one of the most important lunar observatories in Britain," and years later he was proved correct: the Slockavullin stones mark the

Slockavullin.

northernmost and southernmost Major Lunar Standstill every 18.6 years.[4] As a bonus, when the main Templewood stone circle and a nearby recumbent stone are included in the plan, it is possible to calculate the winter solstice, the winter Crossquarter sunrise and the equinoxes. What fascinates me most about this alignment is the way the southern stones are deliberately set into the ground like arrows, at an angle between 19 and 20 degrees. The same is true of standing stones on Mull, as well as one of the main megaliths at the core of Avebury in England. The angle – specifically 19.47° – references the most active hotspots of energy on the faces of the Sun, Venus, Mars, and Jupiter, while on Earth it is marked by Mauna Loa volcano in Hawaii, all at 19.47° latitude.

Simply put, Kilmartin Glen is the promulgation of ideas applied earlier on Orkney and Lewis by people continuing a tried and tested formula.

I made my way to the nearby café that offers a pleasant view of the glen, along with the tastiest soups and the thickest slices of bread for dunking, pored over my notes and took stock of what has been a complex Scottish journey with detours to Sardinia and Armenia.

It is said the Papae and the Peti of Orkney spoke a different language and dressed in a manner that qualified them as a priesthood, setting them apart from other residents. They were expert astronomers and seafarers, taller and of a fair Caucasian complexion. Thanks to a lasting linguistic trail, the Papae can now be identified as the P'apegh of the Armenian

Highlands, whose etymological fingerprint informs us they were elders and holy people who inherited from their ancestors a specialized knowledge and spiritual tradition. Likewise, the Peti come to us via Egyptian and Persian traditions as the Peri, Petiu or Petriu, seers and visionaries concerned with matters pertaining to specific regions of the sky. Their epithet, Shining Ones, formally links them to the Egyptian Aku Shemsu Hor (Shining Ones, Followers of Horus) as well as the Anu-naki of the Armenian Highlands and beyond – secluded groups of astronomer priests, wisdom keepers and temple-builders *par excellence*, whose lineage dates back to antediluvian times, who are known throughout the world by different titles but identical physiognomy and purpose. As we approach the historical period they became known as Tuadhe d'Anu, an elite intimately involved with the Royal House of Scythia.

They arrived in two waves: from the Black Sea region via Scandinavia, and from the Mediterranean via Sardinia. If we follow the general progression of dates offered by the alignment of the sites, they settled on Orkney, then sailed west to the Outer Hebrides and gradually spread south to the Inner Hebrides – Mull, Iona, Arran, Jura – before venturing inland to Kilmartin. There's just one question remaining. Where did they go from here?

A paper by the Indo-European and Celtic scholar Ranko Matasovic describes highly technical features of Old Irish and Insular Celtic language syntax that are "all found in Afro-Asiatic languages, often in several branches of that family, but usually in Berber and Ancient Egyptian." He notes one particular shared feature that "is attested only in the earliest forms of Old Welsh, and it is also not widespread in Afro-Asiatic, occurring only in Old Egyptian and its descendant, Coptic." From his research, Ranko concludes that statistical analysis of parallels between Insular Celtic and Afro-Asiatic "more or less amounts to proof that there was some connection between Insular Celtic and Afro-Asiatic at some stage in prehistory."[5]

The *Historia Brittonum*, a compilation written c.887 AD, describes how the people of Britain and Ireland originated from Scythia. However, the account records a second, southern migration route originating in Egypt, followed by protracted wanderings in the Mediterranean and Iberian Peninsula before their arrival in Ireland. This is affirmed by the latest scientific data, which suggests that by 3200 BC a good portion of the population of Ireland had migrated from the Mediterranean. Their genetic profile indisputably originates in the Middle East, with one woman buried near a stone monument and ring court in Ballynahatty genetically related to the inhabitants of Sardinia.[6] This goes some way to explaining the origin of stones in Ireland carved with circles, ripples and pictograms that are carbon copies of the Mamoaida stone in Sardinia. But there's a twist. Three male skeletons uncovered on the island of Rathlin reveal DNA very different to our woman from Ballynahatty, they have a genetic code that causes blue eyes, and DNA that originated in the steppes of Ukraine and spread westwards through central Europe.[7] Bridging these two identities is the arrival in Ireland of Indo-European language around 4000 BC, coalescing Celtic languages along the Atlantic coastline from southern Iberia to the Shetland Islands via maritime networks.[8]

Furthermore, the analysis of remains from Poulnabrone portal chamber in County Clare reveals the appearance of new genomic DNA signatures by 3800 BC, indicating the arrival of people from elsewhere[9] that coincides with a noticeable elevation in farming techniques, tools, architecture and temple-building. In other words, the arrival of strangers from afar instigated a cultural revolution in Ireland.[10] Since the style of sacred sites is common to those of Carnac, and DNA samples from Neolithic people of Brittany share an Iberian and Mediterranean genetic signature, the general consensus is that the migration trajectory outlined in early historical accounts is supported by a genetic fingerprint.[11]

It may seem counter-intuitive to learn about the prehistory of one nation by examining another's, and yet, with regard to Scotland where so little written information survives, since Ireland contains the richest source of Celtic traditions, it would be foolish not to accept such an invitation. That said, to unravel the prehistory of Ireland is like walking into a shop full of broken china where the shards have been reassembled from totally different pieces resulting in a cornucopia of mismatched crockery. Much like asking for directions and still getting lost. I remember on my first visit being given explicit instructions to a large mound only to arrive an hour later right back beside the person who'd given them. It's an accepted hazard of Ireland's cultural charm.

When it comes to prehistoric records, Ireland possesses the bulk of information, in narratives such as the *Book of Leinster*. Even so, such accounts were copied again and again from remote sources, losing threads along the way, and because most Irish history officially begins with the introduction of Christianity, much of the past has been distorted through the prism of religious idealism, to the point where anything that took place prior to Christianity is generally treated as fantasy. This makes the mounds of the Boyne Valley – Dowth, Knowth and Newgrange, and the evidence of human activity there by 3700 BC[12] – very inconvenient. Compounding the issue is the awkward retelling of ancient stories by compromised early Christian clerics. According to the historian Teresa Cross: "The mythological tales of the old druids of the elder faith, which had been transcribed, were often copied down by clerics who were sometimes embarrassed about the stories these contained regarding the old gods. They would often write prefaces explaining these deities as demons who had fooled the older folk, poor as angels who were not good enough for heaven but were too good for hell."[13] Misplaced romantic antiquarianism further conspired to raise a smokescreen around ancient beliefs and practices, sometimes deliberately, sometimes ignorantly, painting elders and gods alike as noble savages, blurring history with fantastical invention, resulting in the obscurity of fact.

When Julius Caesar invaded Britain, the Roman emperor obsessively amassed a treasure trove of data regarding the origin of its people, writing in *De Bello Gallico* that the ancestor of the Celts was a god who inhabited a distant region beyond the ocean, whose dwelling was in the "far-off islands."[14] Julius' vague reference leads us to assume that no one by then knew the location of these far-off islands, however, the account echoes the description in the *Building Texts* of the early gods of Egypt – the Shining Ones, Followers of Horus – who arrived from the far-off islands Iw Titi and the Island of Fire, with the former speculated to have been in the Indian Ocean. Since the abodes of *all* antediluvian gods appear to have been islands,[15] including the Anu-naki, whose citadel was most likely the island mound Aratta in Armenia, we are left none the wiser. That said, since the period in question was a time of sea levels rising by more than 140 feet it is probable that these places of origin were lost to memory because they had long been lost to the sea. To illustrate the point, there is a description in the earliest British literature, the *Mabinogi*, of Brân the Blessed and his men crossing from Wales to Ireland and how the intervening sea consisted merely of two navigable rivers, the Ili and Archan. The storyteller adds that it is only since then that the sea has multiplied its realms between Ireland and the Isle of the Keiri,[16] which is an accurate observation supported by marine and geological maps: between 10,000-8500 BC the Irish Sea was indeed much narrower and consisted of no more than one or two waterways.[17]

When the Church descended on Ireland the pagan narrative of its history was re-written, re-catalogued and formally incorporated into the 11th century Christianized narrative *Lebor Gabála Érenn* (Book of the Invasions of Ireland). Since the arrival of Ireland's hero Partholón had taken place in prehistoric times, he was irreconcilable with the absurd chronological system established in the Bible, in which the Catholics somehow calculated that a period of just 837 years elapsed between the flood and the exodus from Egypt. If the historical exodus occurred around 1200 BC, and the flood in 9703 BC, immediately there is a discrepancy of 8500 years. Predictably this led to massive blunders, for example, the aforementioned *Book of Leinster*, largely compiled and reassembled by Irish Catholic monks, mentions that no humans lived in Ireland before their date for the flood, making the archaeological evidence of the earliest inhabitants c.8000 BC problematic.[18] Yet a few paragraphs later, the revisionist monks added the legend of Cessair, allegedly a granddaughter of Noah, arriving in Ireland in 2958 BC, forty days *before* the flood, having chosen this island because it was the westernmost point of Europe and thus free from sin, rendering it immune from destruction;

accompanying her were fifty women, three men, and a flock of sheep. Cessair perishes in the deluge along with most of her companions; the first male, Bith, dies soon after, presumably from the pressure of impending copulation and repopulation. The other surviving male, Fintan, by unparalleled miracle lives a further ten thousand years to become a witness in a lawsuit in the 6th century![19] According to the leading 19th century Irish historian, Thomas Moore, Cessair was little more than an invention, and frankly I'm inclined to agree.[20]

Let's then start afresh, with Nennius' 9th century *Historia Brittonum* and the oldest extant manuscript in Irish, *Lebor na hUide* (Book of the Dun Cow), which

place the first people arriving from the Mediterranean in Kenmare Bay after the great flood. Led by the hero Partholón, their tenure in Ireland was challenged by constant shifts in geology, weather, and plagues to which four thousand succumbed within a week.[21] This was a land much different to today's, consisting of just three lakes, nine rivers and one plain where no root or tree was evident,[22] suggesting a region flattened by glaciation and decimated by an upheaval of nature, which was certainly the case during the 3000 years following the Younger Dryas boundary, the period of the flood.[23]

Around 4000 BC, the predecessors of the Gaels and Celts were said to have been governed by descendants of heroes. Such leaders associated with sages who memorialized history, laws, ethics and religion, they honored men and women gifted in the healing arts, magic and divination. But they gave the greatest respect and position to bards and troubadours who, with prodigious memory, recited ancient systems of knowledge handed down through generations, which they wove into song, poetry and other storytelling devices.[24] Thus the mythological gods and the elder faith continued to be retold by a class of professional storytellers. Songs and poems filled with historical and moral trivia would be enacted at Crossquarter festivals such as Samhain and Beltane, while a main event that included kings and queens was performed at the summer solstice at Uisnech, the hill marking the geodetic and sacred center of Ireland.

Throughout the remote past, the epic poetry of troubadours and poets contained historiographical information shedding considerable light on the development of human civilization as well as political, religious and cultural life that would otherwise have been censored by political and religious regimes. In practice, the bards acted as stewards of Wisdom, weaving aged traditions into their stories and songs, making them some the most authoritative, and often the only reliable sources of early history. Their traditions add a piece to Nennius' account, for they all agree that a scribe by the name of Fintan was in fact the progenitor of the Irish, arriving from Mesopotamia prior to the flood.[25] Eight generations from Noah, Partholón and his tribe appear on the scene from Mygdonia, the ancient maritime region of north-eastern Greece bordering Bulgaria[26] – Scythia, by any other name – before settling on an island on the Erne estuary called Inis Samhaoir (pronounced *samar*). It is possible they named it after their place of origin, the river island settlement of Samara to the north of the Black Sea, because Partholón's tribe fits the profile of the people already established there by 5000 BC, who subsequently migrated southwest to what is now Bulgaria and northern Greece, then north via Scandinavia, introducing Proto-Indo-European language as they did, along with the knowledge of building *kurgans*.[27]

Once settled on the Éirne estuary they established a sacred center to the south, around a freestanding coastal massif called Cnoc na Ré, a name visiting Egyptians would find agreeable since Ré happens to be their solar god; on its summit a gigantic *kurgan* transforms the entire hill into a jaw-dropping pregnant belly. In adjacent rolling fields, the settlement of Carrowkeel grew to boast the highest concentration of stone circles, dolmens and passage mounds in Ireland, the only place where all classes of megalithic monuments are found together.

Bardic traditions agree that Partholón's time was marked by notable climatic instability, with unusually high rainfall leading to the bursting of rivers and lakes. Such conditions would have been consistent with those generated around 6200 BC by the rapid switch of North Atlantic thermohaline circulation (the ocean current delivering heat to northern latitudes) and its catastrophic impact on European Neolithic civilization for the next 700 years.[28] The timing is also consistent with the earliest radiocarbon date found at Carrowkeel, 6400 BC.[29]

To add to Partholón's toil, the tribe shared Ireland with the Formorians, a constant source of trouble for them and their successors. The name originates from Old Irish *fo* (under) and *muir* (sea), implying a people whose original abode sank beneath a rising ocean,[30] and quite possibly the source Julius Ceasar was referring to in his account. The Formorians, whose outpost was Tory Island off the coast of Donegal, were depicted as giant, red-haired, deformed humanoids, brutish and crude, known by the epithet 'the Red Ones' and mentioned in the Bible as *nephila*, 'offspring of Orion'. However, the Biblical version, like the revision of Irish prehistory, was altered from the original account written by the antediluvian scribe already familiar to us, Enmed Ur-anu. Enmed describes how a small group of renegade Watchers impregnated human women who begot the *nephila*, and it was their subsequent overrunning of the human race that forced the Lords of Anu to manipulate events that led to the

Cnoc na Re´.

great flood, and in so doing, ironically saved the human race from oblivion.[31] One of the graphic descriptions of the red-haired *nephila* was of their predilection for human flesh, and indeed we find a similar weakness in the Formorians, who exacted tribute from the other residents of Ireland in the form of child slaves.[32]

Next on the scene was Nemed, whose tribe is said to have sailed from the Caspian Sea region of Scythia, an amazing feat considering Nemed would have had to connect to the Black Sea and hence to the Mediterranean. The Caspian Sea is now landlocked, but accounts by early Greek and

Carrowkeel.

Egyptian navigators and merchants indeed suggest there once existed a navigable route from central Asia through the Caspian Sea into the Black Sea that has since vanished due to fluctuation in water levels as well as deviations in the course of the rivers entering these bodies.[33]

Nemed's arrival must have been on the heels of Partholón's people because he too experienced the bursting out of loughs Neath and Éirne, attesting to a land still reacting to inclement climate. Like his predecessor, Nemed also suffered the Formorians. Constantly harassed by them, he left with his son Iarbonel, but instead of taking the easier route south via the English Channel, they opted to sail north via the Outer Hebrides and Orkney, most likely because people of their kind were already established there, along with their respective administrative and religious centers. From Orkney they continued to southern Sweden, settling in Jutland (Denmark) where they impressed Jutlanders with their skills in occult sciences.

After eleven generations practicing magic and divination, Iarbonel's descendants returned to Ireland as the Fir Bolg, meaning 'Men of the Bag',[34] a very telling title since it links them with the sages of Sumeria – and by extension, Scythia – those individuals depicted with a bag known as the *kete* of knowledge. To access the contents of this container is to know the secrets of nature and the motions of the stars and sky as well as the kind of monuments required to hardwire such knowledge on the land – stone circles, passage mounds and all manner of intertwined temples – revealing the type of 'occult sciences' Nemed's descendants were privy to.

Nemed and Partholón's migration route from the Scythian/Armenian territories through the western isles, the time-frame, their seafaring acumen, and the specialist knowledge of *kurgans*, stone circles and related spiritual sciences make them prime candidates for the Neolithic architects of Orkney and Lewis we've been searching for.

And if there is any lingering doubt, the next group to arrive in Ireland will dispel it.

Sardinian spiral carvers appear to have been busy at Aghacarrible, Ireland.

Men of the Bag. Upper Mesopotamia.

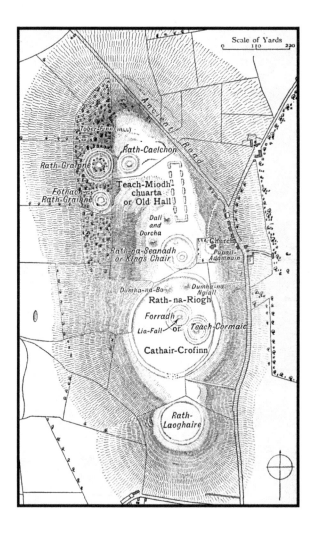

The sacred hill Tara.
Te Ra to an Egyptian.
Ta Ara to an Armenian.

THEY CAME FROM
THE NORTH

t is unanimously claimed in the traditions of Ireland that a group of semi-divine people "descended from the north." Since no one at this time was living in Iceland or the Faroes, we can only assume they came from the direction of Orkney and Lewis. The architects of the Scottish Isles were said to be "strangers from afar" with titles originating in Armenia and Egypt, with historians considering the source of this blonde, tall and fair race to be Finland,[1] having earlier emerged from the Black Sea regions, and followed the Danube River, to which they'd lent their name, *d-anu-be*.[2] Other commentators, such as the Reverend Bede and the 17th century Irish historian Geoffrey Keating, fine-tuned their origins to Greece or Scythia,[3] and as they established a north-western trajectory via Denmark[4] the names of their gods migrated with them, providing a linguistic paper trail.[5] This renowned group of individuals, from whom it was said "men of learning are descended,"[6] was led by one of Nemed's descendents, Boethach, and arrived from Scythia not as Anu-naki or Tuadhe d'Anu, but as Tuatha Dé Danann.[7]

Mythology describes how they acquired occult skills and magical powers from four northern cities called Falias, Murias, Gorias and Finias, except no such cities have ever been found. This isn't a mystery, it is a misunderstanding of old Irish language. The names refer to the four earthly elements: *fail* (understone); *muir* (sea); *gor* (fire); *finn* (white or air) – simply put, earth, water, fire and air, the alchemical foundation of the material world.[8] Following their long residence in the Greek portion of Scythia, the Tuatha Dé Danann became highly skilled in architecture and its associated arts, not to mention teachers of an ancient wisdom that led to the founding of the Druidhe priesthood.[9] In folklore they were considered a race apart, half human half divine,[10] the Lords of Light, always exercising influence over the destiny of humanity, yet living in communities beside but separate from humans. Celtic traditions claim they could make the Sun go dark, implying they were accomplished astronomers who possessed the ability to predict eclipses.[11] Their female custodians of law and culture were called Behn-sidhé (pronounced *banshee*), an Old Irish term meaning 'wise women' who, together with their male counterparts, were masters of the transcendental arts or *sidhé* (pronounced *shee*), known in India as *siddhi*, a wisdom derived from obtaining the highest state of transcendent consciousness. The Druidhe came to refer to it as the Web of the Wise.

Just as in Scythia the Tuadhe d'Anu were described as the 'fair people', so the Tuatha Dé Danann were referred to as *daoine-sidhé*, 'faery folk'. Remembered in Orkney as the Peti, they were known in Persia as Peri, a tall and graceful people possessing the gifts of clairvoyance and the ability to walk between worlds. The name followed them to Ireland where it was modified to reflect the local tongue as *Feadh-Ree*.[12]

At first, this elegant race (the basis for J.R.R. Tolkien's

elegant, bright, shining Elven people of Lothlorien) were ensconced "in the summer isles of the west, where dwelt a divine race of the pure Celtic type, long-faced, yellow-haired hunters, and goddesses with hair like gold,"[13] before following in the footsteps of their ancestors to the already established sacred center at Cnoc na Ré. Radiocarbon dating from the sacred sites in nearby Carrowkeel does indicate a second wave of human activity from 5300 BC to 4200 BC[14] (consistent with the dates of the Orkney sites), with a number of individuals buried there having originated in Asia Minor.[15] This tallies with analysis of mtDNA haplogroups in Ireland with earlier origins in northern Greece, the Black Sea and the Caucasus in 5700 BC, and their presence in Ireland firmly established by 3500 BC.[16]

Once settled, they spread inland into Donegal before landing "on the mountains of Conmaicne Rein in Connacht, bringing a darkness over the Sun for three days and three nights," a romanticized interpretation of the smoke generated from the ritual burning of their

John Duncan's romantic depiction of the Tuatha De'Danann as Riders of the Sidhe'.

ships.[17] Clearly the Tuatha Dé Danann were staying for good.

We have already examined the root of the title Tuadhe d'Anu as *d-anu-na*, meaning 'princely offspring of Anu'.[18] The variant Tuatha Dé Danann comes from the Armenian compound phrase *Tu at'or degh danude'r*, which practically translates as 'you embody the throne and office of the lord', emphasizing their responsibility to uphold an ancient lineage. The word *tuatha* itself migrated into German and Gothic as *thiuda* and *tauta* ('people'), then in Gaulish as *túatha* ('an alliance of several'),[19] before reaching Ireland as *tuath* ('tribe'). Interestingly, in the original Gaelic, *tuath* means 'northward', thus memorializing the direction from which they arrived.[20]

Some bardic traditions claim the Tuatha Dé Danann were Scottish people who moved from the island of Mull to Ireland only a few hundred years before Christ,[21] and although the dating is clearly off by thousands of years, it ought to be remembered that they were the foundation for the Druidhe, which might explain this compression of time. In Ireland the association was maintained between the two by naming the gathering of Druidhe as a *feis*, a term linked to the Gaulish *fée*, or faery, the aphorism by which the Tuatha Dé Danann were known.

Given the prevalence of Armenian language in the naming of places and temples in the western isles of Scotland, I wondered if the same might have prevailed in Ireland, as further validation of the presence of the people of Anu and their influence on the culture in this corner of the world.

We've already seen how the names of Armenian gods begin with Ar, and continue with Ara, Ardi, Aru and so forth. These extend into the Vedic pantheon with the gods Aruna and Aranyan, and in Greek mythology as Artemis and Ares. The prefix *ar* served as a cultural foundation. But as language migrated so did pronunciation and accent, for example, in Sumerian *ar* became *an, anu,*[22] and *ur*. After cultural diffusion took its course, *ar* became *ir*, as in Ir-land,[23] where Anu was wholly adopted as the mother of the Irish gods.[24] And since it was commonplace for kings to derive titles from the gods, it probably comes as no surprise that the Armenian solar god Ardi was adopted in ancient Ireland as Ard-ri, the title of High Kings.

Ireland's original name, Éire, comes from Old Irish, Ériu, and derives from Eriaini, an Armenian goddess whose name defined a settlement and its tribe on the eastern shore of Lake Van.[25] It is also likely that Ireland's fabled Lough Éirne was named for the same goddess, especially as it connects to the island first settled by Partholón and hence the founding of Ireland's prehistory.

We find two principal Armenian deities, Mehr and his consort Armaghan, present in the county of Armagh, an area rich in dolmens and sacred sites, and the Cliffs of Moher, with its folklore of the Tuatha Dé Danann and underwater cities. Moher's Armenian counterpart is Mheri Dur (Mher's Gate), also a cliff beside Lake Van and upon which the names of the gods are inscribed.[26]

In the south of Ireland, the Rock of Cashel became the seat of the historical kings of Munster, although why it was so, out of all possible locations, remains a mystery. The fact that it also became the symbol of Christian power (after St. Patrick forced Satan to spit out part of a mountain that landed on this spot) makes the lack of information on its origins all the more suspicious, to say the least. The Armenian word *kashel* provides a little clarity: it means 'to draw or allure'. Since ancient places were often named after a historical event or purpose, it is likely that a precedent was established for this hill as a focal point for royalty in prehistoric times, much like the Al-thing parliaments of Orkney and Iceland, and the memory of tradition lingered long after the event.

This loose thread was eating away at me, so on a hunch I re-examined another site with similar ties to royal assembly on the opposite side of Ireland in northern Donegal, perhaps the most mysterious part of this land, with its Armenian root *dohm-egan* generally translating as 'distinguished noble clan'. The site in question is Grianán Ailigh, a drum-shaped ring court on the summit of a teardrop hill bearing a passing resemblance to Glastonbury Tor. It is named for the Sun goddess Grainne. Repeatedly rebuilt and restored, this enormous 77-foot inner court encircled by a 14-foot thick wall is a faery ring in every sense of the word, which itself stands within three original stone rings built by Daghda, a fair king of the Tuatha Dé Danann. In the center of the court lies the grave of his son Aedh, an empowering name for someone who had to

Classic faery ring court. Grianán Aliligh.

battle the troublesome giant Formorians, because Áed is Armenian for 'fire'. Hardly surprising this royal court still served as a *rath* for kings in historical times – as must have been the case with the Rock of Cashel.

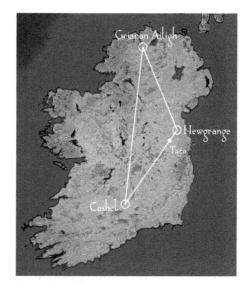

An ancient straight road once linked this faery ring with one of Ireland's main ceremonial places, the Hill of Tara – or the Hill Belonging to Ara, as an Armenian would put it – where the Tuatha Dé Danann placed the sacred stone Lia Fáil, and Lugh, hero and principal figure of the Tuatha Dé Danann, owned an impressive *rath* of his own.

Daghda was allegedly responsible for another site of great significance to the Tuatha Dé Danann, the gigantic passage mound of Newgrange, in whose vicinity stands the romantically named Mound B, a humble *kurgan* where the king is said to be buried.

The striking thing about these sites sharing similar functions (and connected by royal roads) is that Grianán Ailigh and Rock of Cashel lie precisely 100 miles from Newgrange, essentially forming an isosceles triangle across Ireland, where the arm from Newgrange to Cashel passes right through the Rath of Lugh at Tara. It seems the surveyors of Orkney were at also hard at work across Ireland.

The Hill of Tara's counterpart in the northwest is Cnoc na Ré. The area immediately surrounding it features the island's oldest known dolmens, stone circles and passage mounds, confirming the hill's status as the focal point of devotion. In Armenian etymology the phrase *nakh-na-Ara* means 'that which precedes Ara'. At first glance this may look like a case of making words fit a theory, but there is logic behind it. The sky deity Ara is the equivalent of the Egyptian god Ré, whose name is formalized as åa-Ra, 'the domain of Ra'.[27] To precede a god implies a form still in a stage of conception, and nothing depicts this act so vividly as a hill shaped like a pregnant belly.

In turn, Cnoc na Ré's counterpart in the southwest is a mountain called Dá Chich Anann, 'the breasts of Anu', referring to the voluptuous shape of the twin peaks commonly known as Paps of Anu, the visual connotation further enhanced by cairns erected on each summit. The cairns are linked by an ancient ceremonial route, and it is speculated that at least one of them is the ruin of a former passage mound.[28] The Paps of Anu are a fine example of the sky-ground dualism so beloved of ancient people who regarded the sky as the perfection of nature, the domain of the gods, with the mountain serving as the closest point of earthly contact.[29] This is reinforced by the Armenian term *p'ap*, meaning 'belonging to the Earth shore'. If we recall, it is also the term for a grandfather or elder, from which the Papae priests of Orkney derived their name.

The region around the Paps of Anu is rich in standing stones and stone circles, many of them hard to find even with a topographic map, as though their protective spirits enjoy working you hard for an introduction. I recall asking a farmer to help me find one such site. "Oh, ya caan't miss it, just over the brow of da hill, a few minats waak." Forty minutes later across the brow of the hill, the forest, the river, the bog, the mud, the next hill, I finally found my intended destination. At the foot of the Paps, to the northeast, lies its ancient preparatory ring court, a large circular stone enclosure called Cathair Crobh Dearg, 'Seat of the Red Claw'. It is sited on a prominent artificial knoll known as The Shining Hill,[30] yet another reference to the Anu priests, just as in Callanish. The site contains two monoliths aligned to the general direction of the winter solstice, although it is speculated they may have served as uprights for a large dolmen; [31] beside them is an earthen mound, a healing well and a stone altar, all enclosed within a thick, 150-foot diameter stone wall that has suffered poorly from the ravages of religion, need and time. Named after the goddess Crobh Dearg, the ring was known for Beltane rituals and festivities until Catholics put a stop to the fun. People would perambulate the site while reciting prayers and walk their cattle as a purification ritual,[32] all under the motherly protection of the omnipresent Paps of Anu. The two sites are formally linked by a legend of the ring as the mansion of Credhe, the blonde fairy daughter of the King of Kerry,[33] whose presence is still palpable to those who care to attune to their surroundings. As the Celtic aphorism goes, "Heaven and earth are only three feet apart, but in thin places that distance is even shorter."

Three hills, all principal gathering places sacred to the Tuatha Dé Danann. The distance from the Paps of Anu to Cnoc na Ré and Hill of Tara is 154 and 156

Paps of Anu.

miles respectively, a near-perfect isosceles triangle. To demonstrate how the traditions of Ireland and Scotland are interconnected, take the line from Paps of Anu north, bisect the triangle, cross the sea, and it arrives exactly at the ring court on the summit of Dunadd.

The unifying theme behind the sacred places of the people of Anu in Ireland, Orkney and Lewis is continuity between cosmos, land and people for the purpose of maintaining society and the self in harmony. A god in the ancient scheme of things referred to an essence, a spirit form inherent in every element of nature. A stone has a god, a plant has a god, a piece of wood has a god, even electromagnetism is a god. When a person came to understand the essence of a particular facet of nature, he or she became 'as a god'. Thus, gods were 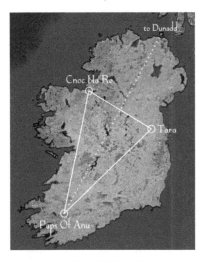 every bit as physical as ordinary people and suffered the cause and effect of the temporal world, but at least they possessed a degree of control over the forces around them. Rituals, traditions, legends, myths, laws and history were learned from a young age, and the knowledge carried by the tribe was cultivated even into adulthood. A woman gifted with prodigious memory was called *badruidhe*; if a man, *druidhe*. It took up to fifteen years to become an *allam*, a 'master of lore', and the seers among them – *uates* if male, *ueledas* or *banfili* if female – understood the power of spells, prayers and incantations, and they possessed the ability of foretelling the future. The same is true of all tribes sharing Indo-European roots. Vedic Indians had their *brahmans*, *adhvarytus* and *udgatyrs*, the Greeks their *hiereos*, the Norse their *godi* and *vitki*.[34]

Society was maintained in equilibrium through a tripartite ideology formalized by a structures of priests and kings, warriors, and farmers, just as it is in the world of gods: priestly gods, warrior gods, and fertility gods. Each reflected the other, and this utopian ideal was desired throughout the social order.

It is for these reasons, above all others, that an enormous effort was undertaken to promulgate and preserve the culture of sacred space, and why individuals sought to export it to difficult and challenging environments. And without it the world would be a hopelessly chaotic place.

Back in Orkney, a soft pink and orange light sheathed Stenness and Loch Harray. A surfacing seal perforated the water, its head sending ripples across the mirror-like surface. Perambulating the stones one more time – there's never enough – I came to appreciate the Irish knack for storytelling, because without it the complete story behind the architects of the stones and mounds of the Scottish Isles would still be wrapped in cultural amnesia. But whatever happened to the Papae, the Peti, the Shining Ones, the people of Anu?

It is said the Tuatha Dé Danann were defeated following a series of wars and subsequently receded into the "hollow hills" – the passage mounds, dolmens and *kurgans* – henceforth remembered as elven folk. They were supplanted by the fair-haired Milesians, descendants of a Scythian noble who was expelled from Egypt and emigrated to northern Iberia, specifically the Basque country,[35] a tradition supported by a genetic study that shows the ancient Irish and Scots carry the same Y-chromosome variation as that of the Basques.[36] But to understand the true fate of the Tuatha Dé Danann we must travel forward to around 400 AD, just as Paladius and other holy men begin introducing Catholicism into Ireland.

Much of the Church's claim to rule by hallowed appointment rests with a fraudulent document called *The Donation of Constantine*, by which it sought all possible means to diminish the status of every strain of the royal bloodline connected to the Anu-naki.[37] Despite all efforts to eradicate it in Europe with the Catholic-backed Carolingian usurpation of power from the Merovingians (whose lineage is traced to the Anu of Sumeria),[38] the Church was horrified to find this bloodline still active when it occupied Ireland. Since the Tuatha Dé Danann were held in high esteem, Irish monks were instructed to come up with a story to eradicate their memory. These physical, semi-divine people needed to be mythologized, not an easy task to accomplish, as the antiquarian Standish O'Grady explains: "So firm was the hold which the ethnic gods of Ireland had taken upon the imagination and spiritual sensibilities of our ancestors that even the monks and Christianized bards never thought of denying them. They doubtless forbade the people to worship them, but to root out the belief in their existence was so impossible that they could not even dispossess their own minds of the conviction that the gods were real supernatural beings."[39]

This much was pointed out in the medieval work *Acallam na Senórach* (Tales of the Elders of Ireland), in which the gods remained powerful long after their alleged defeat by the Milesians. The warrior Caílte mac Rónáin, a survivor of the tribal wars into the days of St. Patrick, declared that the Tuatha Dé Danann must be reduced in power, and he vowed to "relegate them to the foreheads of hills and rocks, unless that now and again thou see some poor one of them appear as transiently he revisits the earth." The victory over the Tuatha is discussed in St. Patrick's *Life*, in which Conn Cruaich ('chief of the mound') and twelve Anu deities bow to Patrick as he raises his crozier and the earth swallows them all, while their spirits, additionally cursed by the saint, flee into the hills and out of sight. But one dialogue between Patrick and Caílte mac Rónáin reveals how the Catholics knew full well the Tuatha Dé Danann were real people whose power derived from understanding the laws of nature, for they speak of them as "fairies with corporeal and material forms, yet imbued with immortality," for which they were referred to as *sidhé*, and which the *Book of Armagh* describes as "deos terrenos," *terrestrial* gods, whom the people adored, even in the era of Patrick.[40]

Since the Tuatha Dé Danann were already commonly known by their complexion as the 'fair folk', the Church simply redefined the term 'fair'. They were re-branded in monastic texts as *supernatural* faeries who'd arisen from a pagan agricultural cult of the goddess Danae of Argos,[41] and portrayed as miniature entities with wings relegated to an unseen world, thus diminishing their importance, and with it their place in history, at a stroke making their legacy controllable. As a deterrent, priests were instructed that anyone who dreamt of such faery folk should be judged to be possessed by the devil and forced to atone, as illustrated in the story of *The Sick-Bed of Cuchulainn*, in which a man becomes bilious through possession by the demonic power of the *sidhé*. [42]

Except the *sidhé* is nothing more sinister than the transcendental source accessed by the Tuatha Dé Danann – or anyone in a state of meditation, for that matter. The late Lawrence Gardner succinctly explains this political machination: "In life, when confronted with a seemingly insurmountable problem, one can either submit to the stress and pressure that it causes or, alternatively, one can mentally diminish the problem. This does not mean that the problem goes away, but it can appear less harassing and more controllable. That was precisely what the church did with the Tuatha Dé Danann; they reduced the problem by diminishing the nominal significance of this ancient king tribe and, in so doing, portrayed them as minute figures who were moved to the realm of mythology, causing a parallel diminution of their history, and their proud legacy was lost from the stage of Western education." [43]

The Church's propaganda machine initially linked faeries to vampires, claiming that the little winged creatures would suck a sleeper's blood (even consumption was defined as a sign of faeries stealing your soul) for which it invented all manner of remedies and charms. Faeries were also blamed for kidnapping the weak who'd strayed from ecclesiastical doctrine. [44]

But still this diminishing of once powerful gods was not enough. Because the Tuatha Dé Danann had conquered earlier races and possessed supernatural skills seemingly beyond mortal men, the story surrounding the Milesians also required reinvention. The newcomers had to overcome the Tuatha, with the misfortunate side effect of artificially pushing back their ancestry some 2000 years. [45] Regardless, Ireland could now be seen under human command long before the arrival of Christianity, with Patrick as a natural

Queen's naga or serpent raft. Siam 1890.

successor. And the more the gods became associated with mounds, the easier it became for propagandists to push a legend of an insurmountable people capable of being defeated by mortals. A classic case of the mythologizing and distortion of fact to ensure the subjugation of a nation by an invasive religion.[46]

In the end, popular history expounds a myth of Patrick ridding Ireland of all snakes, for which he is awarded sainthood, a claim that sounds preposterous no matter what your religion or background. Like others of their kind, the Anu were defined as People of the Serpent, a kind of badge of office confirming their ability to work with the laws of nature.[47] When they are said to have arrived in the green isle "having flown across the ocean on a magical raft of serpents,"[48] it does not imply these people *literally* shared a boat filled with snakes, because the same was said of Quetzalcoatl and his Kaanul (People of the Serpent) when they arrived on the shores of Yucatan.[49] In 'ridding Ireland of snakes' the Church was merely sending a clear political signal that it had snuffed out the divine bloodline for good. Or so they believed.

From that point the "fair people" were relegated to the "hollow hills," and as far as the brainwashed are concerned, they reside there still. But ask any Irish person who is connected to the land and its subtle ways and rhythms and they'll look at you with a sly grin.

Along with a nod and a wink.

In 1833 the Scottish travel writer Constance Frederica described her visit to this 'Great Dragon mound' on Loch Nell as "wonderfully perfect in anatomical outline… the whole length of the spine was carefully constructed with regularly and symmetrically-placed stones at such an angle as to throw off rain," and featuring a long, narrow causeway "made of large stones, set like the vertebrae of some huge animal." On the head mound she found a circle of stones "exactly corresponding with the solar circle as represented on the head of the mystic serpents of Egypt and Phoenicia."

Once known as Tomb of the Finnfolk, this ritual site of the People of the Serpent is now mostly obliterated and overgrown.

NOTES AND BIBLIOGRAPHY

CHAPTER 1

1. CAMS 1946 Royal Commission on the Ancient and Historical Monuments of Scotland, Inventory of the Ancient Monuments of Orkney and Shetland. Edinburgh, p. 302-3

2. Ritchie, Graham. The Stones of Stenness, Proceedings of the Society of Antiquaries of Scotland 107, 1976, p.10; some claim twelve stones, but there is no hard evidence that an extra stone existed

3. Spence, M.. 'Reports of District Secretaries, Renovation and Preservation of the Standing Stones, Stenness', Saga Book Viking Club, 5, 1906, p.62, 253; Ritchie, Graham, The Stones of Stenness, Proceedings of the Society of Antiquaries of Scotland 107, 1976, p.9

4. Ritchie, A., Prehistoric Orkney, Historic Scotland, 1995

5. Burl, A., Stone Circles of the British Isles, Yale University Press, New Haven, 1976, p.101, 211; Scarre, Chris, Neolithic Orkney in its European Context, MacDonald Research Monograph, Cambridge, 2000, p.42

6. Burl, op cit, p.153

7. Pococke, Richard, Tours in Scotland, 1747, 1750, 1760, Kemp, D W (ed), Scottish History Society, Edinburgh, 1887, p.144

8. Low, George. A Tour through the Islands of Orkney and Schetland in 1774, Kirkwall, 1879, xxvi;

Robertson, J. D. M.. An Orkney Anthology: The Selected Works of Ernest Walker Marwick, Vol 1, Scottish Academic Press: Edinburgh, 1991

9. Principal Gordon, Archaeologia Scotica, Vol I, 1792

10. Black, G. F. County Folklore, Orkney and Shetland, Vol III, 1903

11. Sparavigna, Amelia. Megalithic Quadrangles and the Ancient Astronomy, SSRN Electronic Journal, November 2016; Heath, Robin. Sun, Moon & Stonehenge, Bluestone Press, Cardigan, 1998; Silva, Freddy. Avebury's Mysterious Rectangle, www.invisibletemple. com/extra/avebury-square-star-alignments.html

12. Tudor, John. The Orkneys and Shetland, Edward Stanford, London, 1883, p.21

13. Historia Norwegiae; Barry, G. History of the Orkney Islands, Longman, London, 1808, p.115

CHAPTER 2

1. Long, D., Wickham-Jones, C., and Ruckley, N.A., Studies In The Upper Palaeolithic of Britain and Northwest Europe, S296, 1986, p.55-62

2. ibid

3. www.orkneyjar.com/ archaeology/2008/03/20/new-contender-for-orkneys-oldest-settlement-site/

4. "Hazelnut shell pushes back date of Orcadian site", Stone Pages

Archaeo News, Nov 3, 2007
5. The Storegga Slide
6. Davidson, J.L., and Henshall, A.S. The Chambered Cairns of Orkney, Edinburgh University Press, Edinburgh, 1989, p.12-14
7. Heath, Robin. Sun, Moon and Stonehenge, Bluestone Press, Cardigan, 1998, p.56
8. Thom, Alexander, Megalithic Rings, British Series 81, 1980
9. Renfrew, Colin, Investigations in Orkney, Thames & Hudson, London, 1979, p.213
10. Mercer, S.A.B., Religion in Ancient Egypt, London, 1946, p.121; Goyon, Georges. Les Secrets des Batisseurs des Grandes Pyramides: Kheops, Pygmalion, Paris, 1991, p.89-92
11. Richards, Colin, Building The Great Stone Circles of the North, Windgather Press, Oxford, 2013, p.98-100, 109-112
12. Thom, A., and Thom, A.S., Megalithic Remains in Britain and Brittany, Clarendon Press, Oxford, 1978

CHAPTER 3
1. Thomas, F.W.L. et al. Account of some of the Celtic Antiquities of Orkney, Archaeologia, 34(1), 1851
2. ibid
3. Bournemouth Daily Echo, 10th June 2005
4. Silva, Freddy. The Divine Blueprint, Invisible temple, 2012, p.219-236
5. Petrie, George. The Picts' houses in the Orkneys. Archaeological Journal, 20(1), 1863, p.32-37
6. Card, N. et al. Excavation of Bookan chambered cairn, Sand-wick, Orkney. in Proceedings of the

Society of Antiquaries of Scotland, Vol. 135, 2005, pp. 163-190
7. "Hazelnut shell pushes back date of Orcadian site", Stone Pages Archaeo News, Nov 3, 2007
8. Bauval, Robert, and Gilbert, Adrian. The Orion Mystery, Crown, New York, 1994

CHAPTER 4
1. Wikham-Jones, C., et al, Drowned Stone Age Settlement in the Bay of Firth, 2009
2. Barnes, M.. The Interpretation of the Runic Inscriptions of Maeshowe. Viking Age in Caithness, Orkney and the North Atlantic. Edinburgh University Press, 1993
3. Petrie, G.. Letter to The Orcadian newspaper. July 20, 1861; Thomas, F.W.L. Account of some of the Celtic Antiquities of Orkney, Archaeologia, 34(1), 1851
4. Govedarica, Blagoje. Conflict or Coexistence: Steppe and Agricultural Societies in the Early Copper Age of the Northwest Black Sea Area, 2016; Kipfer, Barbara Ann. Encyclopedic Dictionary of Archaeology, Springer, 2000, p.291
5. Bayliss, A., Marshall, P., et al. Islands of History: The Late Neolithic Timescape of Orkney. Antiquity, 91(359), 2017, p. 1171–1188
6. Challands, A., Muir, T. and Richards, C.. The Great Passage Grave of Maeshowe. In Richards, C. (ed). Dwelling among the monuments: the Neolithic village of Barnhouse, Maeshowe passage grave and surrounding monuments at Stenness, McDonald Institute for Archaeological Research,

Cambridge, 2005, pp. 229–248
7. Le Rouzic, Zacharie.
Restaurations faites dans la région
de Carnac. Chambre dolménique
de Kercadoret, commune de
Locmariaquer, Ch. Monnoyer, Le
Mans, 1931
8. Petrie, G. Letter to The Orcadian,
July 20, 1861
9. Bayliss, op cit
10. Challands, op cit

CHAPTER 5
1. Barry, G., History of the Orkney
Islands, Longman, Hurst, Rees and
Orme, London, 1808, p.99
2. Barber, John, The Excavation
of a Stalled Cairn at the Point
of Cott, Westray, Scottish Trust
For Archaeological Research
Monograph, Edinburgh, 1997
3. Ashmole, Patrick. A Radiocarbon
Database for Scottish Archaeological Samples, Radiocarbon, Vol. 42,
1, Glasgow, 2000
4. Hibbert, Samuel. Tings of
Orkney and Shetland, Archaeologia
Scotia, 111, 1831, p.103-210
5. Tudor, John. The Orkneys
and Shetland, Edward Stanford,
London, 1883, p.20-21
6. Michell, John. The Sacred
Center, Inner Traditions, Rochester,
2009, p.49-50
7. ibid
8. Palsson, Einar. The Roots
of Icelandic Culture, Mimir,
Reykjavik, 1986
9. Newham, C.A.. The
Astronomical significance of
Stonehenge, Coates & Parker,
2000; Richards, J.. Stonehenge,
English Heritage Guidebooks,
2013, p.4–7
10. ie. Michell, John. The New

View Over Atlantis, Thames &
Hudson, London, 1982; Silva,
Freddy. The Divine Blueprint,
Invisible Temple, 2012, p. 47, 134
11. Silva, Freddy. The Divine
Blueprint, Invisible Temple,
Portland, 2010, p.134 ibid
12. Gordon, E.O.. Prehistoric
London, Covenant Publishing,
London, 1946
13. Barnes, Michael. The Norn
Language, Gardners Books, 1998
14. Historia Norwegiae
15. ibid; Barry, George. History
of the Orkney Islands, Longman,
London, 1808, p.115
16. Book of Enoch
17. Keay, J.. Collins Encyclopaedia
of Scotland, HarperCollins,
London, 1994
18. Reymond, E.R.E.. The Mythical
Origin of the Egyptian Temple,
Manchester University Press, 1967
19. Budge. E.A. Wallis. An Egyptian
Hierogliphic Dictionary, John
Murray, London, 1920, p.245, 238
20. Sykes, B. Blood of the
Isles, Bantam Books: London,
2006, p.212
21. Oppenheimer, S. The Origins of
the British: a genetic detective story.
Constable: London, 2006, p.152
22. Moffat, Alistair. Britain's DNA
Journey, Birlinn Ltd, Edinburgh,
2013

CHAPTER 6
1. Wickham-Jones, Caroline.
Footsteps in the North, in From
Bann Flakes to Bushmills, Findlay,
Nyree (ed) et al. Oxbow Books,
Oxford, 2009, ch.16
2. Cummings, C.F. Gordon, In The
Hebrides, Chatto and Windus,
London 1883, p.59

3. Herodotus VII, 73; Borza, Eugene. In The Shadow of Olympus, Princeton University Press, Princeton, 1990 p.65

4. Pokorny, Julius. Indogermanisches Etymologisches Woerterbuch, University of Leiden, 2011, p.140-141

5. Silva, Freddy. The Lost Art of Resurrection, Invisible Temple, Portland, 2014

6. Ponting, Margaret and Gerald Curtis, Bernera Bridge: Discovery and Excavation in Scotland, 1985

7. ie. Becker and Selden, The Body Electric, William Morrow, New York, 1998; McTaggart, Lynne. The Field, HarperCollins, New York, 2008, p.109-122; Radin, Dean, and Nelson, Roger. Evidence for consciousness-related anomalies; and 'When immovable objections meet irresistible evidence, Behavioral and Brain Sciences, 1987, 10: 600-1

8. Ashmole, Patrick. 1995, p.31; Silva, Freddy. The Lost Art of Resurrection, Invisible Temple, Portland, 2014, p.76

9. Local historian Margaret Curtis made the same observation

10. Ponting, Margaret, and Gerald. New Light on the Stones of Callanish, G & M Ponting, Stornoway, 1984; Ponting, Margaret, and Gerald. Decoding The Callanish Complex, in D. Heggie (Author), Archaeoastronomy in the Old World, Cambridge University Press, Cambridge, 1982 p. 191-204

11. Richards, Colin. Building The Great Stone Circles of the North, Windgather Press, Oxford, 2003, p.256

12. ibid, p.270 citing Coles, Rees. 1993, 1994, 1995

13. Devereux, Paul. The Ley Hunter, Center for Earth Mysteries Studies, Brecon, Summer/Autumn 1986, p.4

14. ie. Merreux, Pierre. Des Pierres Pour Les Vivants, Nature & Bretagne, Kerwangwenn, 1992

15. Silva, Freddy. The Missing Lands, Invisible Temple, 2019, p.88-91

16. Richards, op cit, p.290

17. Anderson, Joseph. Scotland In Pagan Times, David Douglas, Edinburgh, 1883, p.192

18. In mainland Scotland duns are referred to as brochs

CHAPTER 7

1. Brittannicarum Ecclesiarum Antiquitates

2. Elder, Isabel Hill. Celt, Druid and Culdee, Covenant Publishing Co., 1938

3. Stewart, Alexander. History of Fortingall, A. Maclaren, Glasgow, 1928

4. Bevan-Jones, Robert. The ancient yew: a history of Taxus baccata, Windgather Press, Bollington, 2004

5. Lewis, Samuel. Topographical Dictionary of Scotland, Institute of Historical Research.1846, pp. 526–46

6. see Silva, Freddy. First Templar Nation, Invisible Temple, Portland, 2015

7. My thanks to Lorne Maclaine for putting me in touch with local historian George Sassoon and his unpublished research.

8. McNie, Alan. Your Scottish Heritage, Cascade Publishing, 1983, p.9-11

9. Moy Castle Report, August 1971
10. ie. Silva, Freddy. First Templar Nation, Invisible Temple, Portland, 2016
11. McClenechan, C.. The Book of the Ancient & Accepted Scottish Rite of Freemasonry, Masonic Publishing Co, 1884, p.223
12. Beaumont, Comyns. The Riddle of Prehistoric Britain, Rider, London, 1945, p.168
13. Hay, George. History of Arbroath to the Present Time, Thomas Buncle & Co., Arbroath, 1899, p.474
14. Silva, Freddy. The Lost Art of Resurrection, Invisible Temple, Portland, 2014
15. ibid
16. ibid
17. Cummings, C.F. Gordon, In The Hebrides, Chatto and Windus, London 1883, p.63-72
18. Armstrong, Karen. Islam: A Short History, Widenfield & Nicolson, New York, 2002, p.11
19. Hitti, Philip. History of the Arabs, MacMillan, New York, 1937, p. 96-101
20. Cross, Teresa. Secrets of the Druids, Inner Traditions, Rochester, 2020, p.14
21. Wright, Dudley. Druidism the Ancient Faith of Britain, J. Burrow & Co, London, 1924, p.4
22. Higgins, Geoffrey. The Celtic Druids, Rowland Hunter, London, 1829
23. Cummings, op cit
24. Matthews, John, and Green, Marian. The Grail Seeker's Companion, Thorsons, London, 1986
25. Baronius add. ann. 306. Vatican MSS. Nova Legenda

26. Iona Official Guide, published by Historic Scotland, 2018
27. The Psalter of St. Columba
28. Silva, Freddy. First Templar Nation, Invisible Temple, Portland, 2016
29. Brydall, Robert. Iona: Its History, Antiquities, etc, Houlston & Sons, London, 1898, p.23-30
30. Eisenman, R., James the Brother of Jesus, Faber & Faber, 1997
31. Silva. The Lost Art of Resurrection, op cit
32. Pennant, Thomas. A Tour In Scotland and Voyage to the Hebrides, Benjamin White, London, 1774, p.297
33. Gardner, Laurence. Genesis of the Grail Kings, Element, Boston, 2000, p.46
34. ie, Herouni, Paris. Armenians and Old Armenia, Tigran Mets, Yerevan, 2004, p.170-3
35. Charles, E.H, trans. The Book of Enoch, Society for Promoting Christian Knowledge, London, 1917, Ch. LXXI, p.60
36. Jubilees 4: 16-18, and 8:3; Laurence, Richard, trans. The Book of Enoch, John Henry Parker, Oxford, 1838, p.84-97

CHAPTER 8

1. Guido, Margaret. Ancient People and Places, Thames & Hudson, London, 1963, p.30
2. Tel el Amarna letters c.1300 BC
3. Centini, Andrea. Molecular Biology and Evolution, vol 34, 2, 14 Feb. 2017
4. Guido, op cit, p.31
5. ibid
6. Muscas, Luigi. The Giants of Sardinia, Il Libro, Sanluri, 2019, p.14

7. ibid, p.98
8. ibid, p.63
9. ibid, p.21-22
10. ibid, p.97
11. Reuters. The Lethbridge Herald, AB 31 Oct 1953, p4
12. Muscas, op cit, p.25, 29
13. ibid, p.89
14. ibid, p.90-1
15. ibid, p.104
16. ibid, p.99
17. Hastings, J., and Selbie, J., eds. Encyclopaedia of Religion and Ethics, Charles Scribner's Sons, New York, 1910, vol. II, p.513
18. Hoskin, Michael, et al. The Tombe Di Giganti and Temples of Nuraghic Sardinia, Archaeoastronomy, no. 18, Science History Publications, 1993, S1-26
19. ie. Silva, Freddy. The Divine Blueprint, Invisible Temple, Portland, 2009, p.177-192; Miller, Hamish, and Broadhurst, Paul. The Sun and the Serpent, Pendragon Press, 1990
20. Muscas, op cit. p.5
21. Silva, Freddy. The Missing Lands, Invisible Temple, Portland, 2019
22. Bouchier, E.S. Sardinia In Ancient Times, HH Blackwell, Oxford, 1917, p.8
23. Tyndale, John. The Island of Sardinia, Vol I, Richard Bentley, London, 1849, p.110
24. Guido, op cit, p.109
25. ibid, p.110, 123
26. Tyndale, op cit, p.116
27. Muscas, op cit, p.36, 94
28. Tyndale, op cit, p.112
29. Bauval, Robert, and Gilbert, Adrian. The Orion The Orion Mystery, Crown, New York, 1994
30. Zedda, Mauro. Astronomia Nella Sardinia Preistorica, Agora Nuragica, Cagliari, 2013, p.145
31. Muscas, op cit, p.84
32. ibid, p.37
33. ibid. p.261
34. ibid, p.84
35. Silva. The Missing Lands, op cit, p.177
36. Abela, Giovanni Francesco. Della Descrittione di Malta isola nel Mare Siciliano, Paolo Bonacotaand, Malta, 1647
37. Silva, op cit, p.171-182
38. Ulogini. Luigi. Malta: Origini della Civilita Mediterranea, La Libreria dello Stato, Rome, 1934, p.244
39. My thanks to Armenian researcher Maral Nersessian for clarifying this etymology. nuiragan/ nouiragan pronounced nviragan; nuirag/nvirag
40. Kavoukjian, Martiros. Armenia, Subartu and Sumeria, Montreal, 1987, p.4
41. Silva, Freddy. The Lost Art of Resurrection, Invisible Temple, Portland, 2016, p.147-8
42. Kavoukjian, op cit, p.159
43. ibid p.165
44. Wade, Nicholas. "Date of Armenia's Birth, Given in 5th Century, Gains Credence, New York Times, March, 10, 2015
45. Weninger, Bernhard, et al. Climate Forcing Due to the 8200 Cal yr BP Event Observed at Early Neolithic Sites in the Eastern Mediterranean, Quaternary Research, 66 (3), 401-420, 2006
46. Frisia, Silvia, et al. Holocene Climate Variability in Sicily from a Discontinuous Stalagmite Record and the Mesolithic to Neolithic Transition, Quaternary Research,

66 (3), August 2006
47. Roberts, N., et al. The mid-Holocene climatic transition in the Mediterranean: Causes and consequences, Sage journal, January 25, 2011

CHAPTER 9
1. MacBain, Alexander. Etymological Dictionary of Scottish-Gaelic, Eneas Mackay, Stirling, 1911 p.i-ii
2. Jackson, K.H., in Wainright, F.T., The Problem of the Picts, Melven Press, Perth, 1980, p.142
3. Torosyans, Hakob and Levon. German-Armenian Dictionary, Beirut, 1987, i-iv
4. Cavalli-Sforza, Luigi. Genes, Peoples and Languages, North Point Press, New York, 2000, p.159-165; Gray, R., and Atkinson, Q. "Language-tree divergence times support the Anatolian Theory of Indo-European origin", Nature, vol. 426, Nov. 26, 2003, 435-439; Bouckaert, Remco, et al. Mapping the Origins and Expansion of the Indo-European Language Family, Science, Vol. 337, 6097, 2012, p.957-960
5. Ruhlen, Merritt. The Origin of Language, John Wiley & Sons, New York, 1994
6. Herouni, Paris. Tigran Mets, Yerevan, 2004, p.169
7. Kavoukjian, Martiros. Armenia, Subartu and Sumeria, Montreal, 1987, p.120
8. Lubicz, R.A. Schwalleer de. Sacred Science, Inner Traditions, Vermont, 1982, p.111
9. Herouni, op cit, p.171-3
10. King, Leonard William, et al. Egypt and Western Asia in the Light of Recent Discoveries, Society for Promoting Christian Knowledge, London, 1907, p.384
11. Petrie, Flinders. Society for Promoting Christian Knowledge, London, 1907, p.384
12. Budge, E.A. Wallis. Dictionary of Egyptian Hieroglyphs, J. Murray, London, 1920, p.390, 585, 613, 629, 706, 711, 715
13. Scranton, Laird. The Mystery of Scara Brae, Inner Traditions, Rochester, 2016, p.82
14. Budge, p.15, 237
15. Budge, op. cit, p.15
16. Scranton op. cit, p.31-5
17. ibid
18. cited Kavoukjian, op cit, p.158
19. Khorenatsi, Movses. The History of Armenia, Yerevan, 1981, I-9, 10. In later Hellenistic times he assumes the duty of a fire deity, representing the volcanic nature of the region.
20. It must be stressed that the first king of the country officially known as Armenia, Hayk, borrowed his name from the constellation that defined his territory. Thus the 'people of Hayk' carries two meanings.
21. Setyan, Vahan. Armenian Origins of Basque, 2017, p.99
22. Cross, Teresa. Secrets of the Druids, Inner Traditions, Rochester, 2020, p.107
23. Scranton, op cit, p.43
24. Herouni, op cit, p.164
25. www.canmore.org.uk/site/4170/lewis-garynahine-tursachan
26. Budge, pop cit, .644
27. Silva, Freddy. The Missing Lands, Invisible Temple, Portland, 2019
28. Setyan, op cit

29. Airborne laser scan reveals
Arran's 1,000 ancient sites. BBC
News, 10 October 2019
30. Bryce, T. On the Cairns
of Arran - a Record of further
Explorations during the Season of
1902. Proceedings of the Society of
Antiquaries of Scotland, 37, 1903,
p.36-67
31. Later adopted as a protector
God of War during the Urartian
Kingdom of Van
32. Bede. Historia Ecclesiastica
Gentis Anglorum; Annals of Ulster;
Labor na hUidre; Walafrid Strabo

CHAPTER 10
1. Khorenatsi, Movses. The History
of Armenia, Yerevan, 1981
2. Kavoukjian, Martiros. Armenia,
Subartu and Sumer, Montreal,
1987, p.1, 19
3. Herouni, Paris. Armenians and
Old Armenia, Tigran Mets, Yerevan,
2004 p.171, 212
4. Kavoukjian, op cit, p.101;
Setyan, Vahan. Armenian Origins of
Basque, 2017, p.47
5. Herouni, op cit, p.149
6. Kavoukjian, op cit, p.3, 16
7. ibid, p.82
8. ibid, p.18
9. ibid, p.4
10. ibid, p.172; Kramer, The
Sumerians, University of Chicago
Press, 1963, p.80, 87
11. Gelb, Ignace. Hurrians and
Subarians, University of Chicago
Press, 1944, p.40
12. Kroonen, Guus, et al.
"Linguistic supplement to
Damgaard: Early Indo-European
languages, Anatolian, Tocharian
and Indo-Iranian", Zenodo, 9 May
2018, 3

13. Kavoukjian, op cit, p.4-5
14. Douglas-Klotz, Neil. Kahlil
Gibran's Little Book of Lofe,
Hampton Roads Publishing, 2018,
p. xiv
15. ie. Rigveda, I-10, 31, 130; II-
20, 24; III-5, 59
16. ie. Peder Steffensen, Jorgen.
N.I.B. Center for Ice and Climate,
University of Copenhagen, 11 Dec
2008
17. Herouni, op cit, p.50
18. Kavoukjian, op cit, p.73-4
19. Ghafadaryan, Karo. Armenian
Soviet Encyclopedia, Vol I,
Armenian Academy of Sciences.
1974, pp. 407–412
20. Gelb, op cit, p.43
21. Hallo, W, and Simpson, W..
The Ancient Near East, New York,
1971, p.21; Kavoukjian, op cit,
p.94
22. Herouni, op cit, p.34
23. Petrosyan, Armen, and
Bobokhyan, Arsen. The Vishap
stelae, National Academy of
Sciences of Armenia, Yerevan,
2015; Piotrovsky, Boris. Vishaps.
Stone statues in the mountains of
Armenia, 1939
24. ibid
25. Purschwitz, Christoph.
Chalcolithic and Middle Bronze
Age obsidian industries at Karmir
Sar: A mountain view on the
lithic economies of the Southern
Caucasus. Free University of
Berlin, Institute of Near Eastern
Archaeology, Berlin, 2018, p.23-25
26. Herouni, op cit, p.9-38
27. ibid, p.48
28. ibid, p.53; Brooker, Charles.
Magnetism and Standing Stones,
New Scientist, January 13, 1983
29. Herouni, op cit, p.27

30. Bochkarev N.G., Bochkarev Yu.N. Armenian Archaeoastronomical Monuments Carahunge and Metsamor, Report on International Conference on Archaeoastronomy, SEAC-IO, Tartu, 2002. Reprint in Folklor, Tartu, 2003; Herouni, op cit, p.44
31. Budge, E.A. Wallis. Egyptian Hieroglyphic Dictionary, Vol I, John Murray, London, 1920, p.15
32. Prag, Kay. The 1959 Deep Sounding at Harran in Turkey, Levant 2, 1970, p.71-2
33. Charles, R.H.. The Book of Jubilees, Adam and Charles Black, London, 1902, p.71-2
34. Hassam, Selim. Excavations at Giza, Vol. IV, Government Press, Cairo, 1948, p.45
35. Hancock, G., and Bauval, R. The Message of the Sphinx, New York, 1996, p.4
36. Teryan, op cit, p.7; Kavoukjian, op cit, p.55, 114, 117
37. Herouni, op cit, p. 176
38. Von Furer-Haimendorf, Christof. Megalithic Rituals Among The Gadabas and Bondos of Orisa, Journal of Asiatic Society of Bengal, 9, 1943, p,173
39. Silva, Freddy. The Missing Lands, Invisible Temple, Portland, 2019, p.46-50
40. Kavoukjian, op cit, p.96, 137; Gelb, op cit, p.20
41. Silva, op cit
42. Makere and Te Porohau Ruka Te Korako, comp. Barry Brailsford. Whispers of the Waitaha, Wharakiki Publishing, Christchurch, 2006, p.29, 199-200
43. Silva, op cit

CHAPTER 11

1. Anglo-Saxon Chronicle, c.890 AD, p.1
2. Giles, J.A., ed.. The Miscellaneous Works of Venerable Bede: Ecclesiastical History, vol. II, William Stevens, London, 1843, p.32-33
3. Teryan, Angela. Ancient Written Sources of European Nations About Their Ancestral Homeland Armenia and Armenians, Voskan Yerevantsi, Yerevan, 2017, p.74
4. Herouni, Paris. Armenians and Old Armenia, Tigran Mets, Yerevan, 2004, p.128
5. Goslin, Jérôme, et al. A new Holocene relative sea-level curve for western Brittany, Quaternary Science Reviews 129:341-365, December 2015
6. Herouni, op cit, p.199
7. Budge, E.A. Wallis. Egyptian Hieroglyphic Dictionary, p.29, 129, 804
8. As Gyumri. Herouni, op cit, p.204
9. Kavoukjian, Martiros. Armenia, Subartu and Sumeria, Montreal, 1987, p.128
10. Herouni, op cit, p.204
11. ibid, p.34, 176
12. Armenian Soviet Encyclopedia, Vol. I, 1974, p.379
13. cited Kavoukjian, op cit, p.158
14. Silva, Freddy. The Missing Lands, Invisible Temple, Portland, 2019, p.213-228
15. Gardner, Laurence, Realm of the Ring Lords, Fair Winds Press, Gloucester, 2002, p.52
16. ibid
17. Charles, R. H. Book of the Secrets of Enoch, Oxford, 1896, XXI:2-XXII:12
18. Manetho, The Aegyptica of

Manetho, Harvard University Press, 1940, p.3-5

19. Wilkinson, J. Gardner. The Hieratic Papyrus of Turin, T. Richards, London, 1851; Schwaller de Lubicz, R.A., Sacred Science, the King of Pharaonic Theocracy, Inner Tradition International, New York, 1982, p.87

20. O'Brien, Christian, and Joy, Barbara. The Genius of the Few, Dianthus, Cirencester, 1997, p.27

21. Gardner, op. cit., p.25

22. Charles, op cit

23. Pliny bk VI, chXVII

24. Roux, G.. Ancient Iraq, Allen & Unwin, London, 1964, p.75

25 Movsisyan, Artak. Armenia in the 3rd millennium BC, Nat. Academy of Sciences, Yerevan, 2005

26. Gardner, Laurence. Genesis of the Grail Kings, Element, Boston, 2000, p.161; Movsisyan, Artak. The Writing Culture of Pre-Christian Armenia, Yerevan University, Yerevan, 2006, p.36; Gardner, Realm of the Ring Lords, op. cit., p.68-9

27. Roux, op cit

28. Gardner, op. cit, p.6, 58

29. Herodotus. The Histories, Oxford U. Press, 1998, book 4, items 21, 57, 117

30. Gardner, op cit, p.32, 91, 110

31. Newark, Tim, and McBride, Angus. Barbarians, Concord Publishing, Hong Kong, 1998, p.24

32. Govedarica, Blagoje. Conflict or Coexistence: Steppe and Agricultural Societies in the Early Copper Age of the Northwest Black Sea Area, 2016; Kipfer, Barbara Ann. Encyclopedic Dictionary of Archaeology, Springer, 2000, p.291;

Piotrovsky, Boris, et al. "Excavations and Discoveries in Scythian Lands", in From the Lands of the Scythians: Ancient Treasures from the Museums of the U.S.S.R., 3000 B.C.–100 B.C. The Metropolitan Museum of Art Bulletin, v. 32, no. 5, 1974

33. Silva, Freddy. The Lost Art of Resurrection, Invisible Temple, Portland, 2014, p.51

34. Anthony, David. The Horse, the Wheel, and Language: How Bronze-Age Riders from the Eurasian Steppes Shaped the Modern World, Princeton University Press, 2007

35. Gardner, Laurence, Realm of the Ring Lords, op cit, p.68

36. Keyser, Christine, and Bouakaze, Caroline, et al. Ancient DNA provides new insights into the history of south Siberian Kurgan people, Human Genetics: scientific journal, ed. David N. Cooper, Thomas J. Hudson, Springer Science + Business Media, 2009, Vol. 126, fasc. 3, p.395-410

37. Gardner, op cit, p.100

38. ibid p.109; Budge, op cit, p.238

39. Gardner, ibid

40. Craw, J.H. Excavations at Dunadd, Proceedings of the Society of Antiquaries of Scotland 64: 111-126, 1930

41. Skene, William. The Coronation Stone, Edinburgh, 1869; Keating, Geoffrey. The History of Ireland, Vol I, Irish Texts Society, London, 1902, p.223; Gerber, Pat. Stone of Destiny, Canongate Books, 1997

42. Duncan, Archibald. Scotland, the Making of a Kingdom, Oliver & Boyd, Edinburgh, 1978. There is

a conflicting story that, on the way to Scotland, it was taken to Iona by Columba, although it ought to be pointed out that the account was written posthumously by the Christian evangelist Adamnam who painted Columba's life as pre-destined in the Bible, even juxtaposing the experiences of biblical characters onto the saint to further inflate his image. Since Columba himself was not a king, nor was he of royal blood, it is safe to assume the Lia Fáil never set foot on Iona

43. Muscas, Luigi. The Giants of Sardinia, Il Libro, Sanluri, 2019, p.93
44. The Annals of Ulster
45. The margin of error is 5°

CHAPTER 12
1. Thom, Alexander. Megalithic Lunar Observatories, Oxford University Press, London, 1971, p.37
2. Haddington, Evan. University of Oklahoma Press, Norman, Early Man and the Cosmos, 1984, p.57
3. Scott, J.G.. The stone circle at Temple Wood, Kilmartin, Argyll. Archaeological Journal 15: 53-124, Glasgow 1988-1989
4. Thom, A., A.S. Thom & H.A.H. Burl. Megalithic rings: plans and data for 229 monuments in Britain, British Archaeological Reports series 81, Oxford, 1980
5. Wuethrich, Bernice. Learning The World's Languages Before They Vanish, Science, Vol. 298, issue 5469, May 19, 2000
6. Cassidy, Lara, Martiniano, Rui, et al. Neolithic and Bronze Age ancient Irish genomes, Proceedings of the National Academy of Sciences, Jan 2016, 113 (2) 368-373
7. ibid; Allentoft, et al 2015, Population genomics of Bronze Age Eurasia, Nature 522, 167-172
8. Cunliffe, B. Facing the ocean: the Atlantic and its people. Oxford University Press, Oxford, 2001
9. Cassidy, L. et al. A dynastic elite in monumental Neolithic society, Nature 582, 347-349, 2020; Sheridan, Alison. Nature, 2020-7-4
10. Mallory, J.P.. The Origins of the Irish, Thames & Hudson, London 2013, p.71-103
11. Rivollat, M., et al. Ancient genome-wide DNA from France highlights the complexity of interactions between Mesolithic hunter-gatherers and Neolithic farmers, Science Advances, 29 May 2020, Vol. 6, no. 22
12. Schulting, R.J., et al. New dates from the north, and a proposed chronology for Irish court tombs. Proceedings of the Royal Irish Academy 112C: 1- 60, 2012; Archaeological Inventory of County Meath, Stationery Office, Dublin, 1987, revised 2020
13. Cross, Teresa. Secrets of the Druids, Inner Traditions, Rochester, 2020, p.18
14. VI, ch.XVIII, p.1
15. Silva, Freddy. The Missing Lands, Invisible Temple, Portland, 2019
16. Rhys, John. Celtic Folklore, Welsh and Manx, Vol I, Clarendon Press, Oxford, 1801, p.386; Guest, Lady Charlotte. The Mabinogion, London, 1849, p.35
17. Wingfield, Robin. A model of sea levels in the Irish and Celtic

seas during the end-Pleistocene to Holocene transition, Geographical Society, Special Pubs., London, 96, 209-242, 1 January, 1995; Lambeck, Kurt. Glaciation and sea level change for Ireland and the Irish Sea since late Devensian/Midlandian time, Journal of the Geological Society, London, Vol. 153, 1996, p.853-872

18. Bayliss, A., and Woodman, F., Proceedings of the Prehistoric Society 75, London, 2009, p.101-23

19. Jubainville, H. D'Arbois. Irish Mythological Cycle, Hodges, Figgis & Co, Dublin, 1903, p.36-38

20. Moore, Thomas. History of Ireland, Vol I, Baudry's European Library, Paris, 1837, p.75

21. Giles, J. A. (trans), Nennius' History of the Britons, §13, Six Old English Chronicles, Bohn's Antiquarian Library, 1848

22. Book of Leinster, p.5

23. For example, Moore C.R., Brooks, M.J, et al. "Sediment Cores from White Pond, South Carolina, contain a Platinum Anomaly, Pyrogenic Carbon Peak, and Coprophilous Spore Decline at 12.8 ka". Scientific Reports. 9, 15121, 22 October 2019; University of South Carolina, "Controversial Theory on Extinction of Ice-Age Animals Supported by New Evidence," SciTech Daily, 26 October 2019

24. Cross, op cit, p.7

25. Kennedy, Patrick. Legendary Fictions of the Irish Celts, MacMillan and Co, London, 1866

26. O'Brien, Henry, Phoenician Ireland, Longman & Co, London 1833, p.84

27. Balter, Michael, "Mysterious Indo-European homeland may have been in the steppes of Ukraine and Russia", Science, 13 February 2015

28. Roberts, N., Brayshaw, D., et al. The mid-Holocene climatic transition in the Mediterranean: Causes and consequences, Sage Journals, January 25, 2011

29. Burenhult Göran. Carrowmore: Tombs for Hunters British Archaeology Issue 82

30. Rhys. Hibbert Lectures, cited Squire, Charles. Celtic Myth & Legend, Poetry & Romance, Gresham Pub. Co., 1886, p.48

31. Charles, R.H., ed. The Book of Enoch, Society for Promoting Christian Knowledge, London, 1917; Black, Matthew, ed.. 1 Enoch, E.J. Brill, Leiden, 1985

32. Jubainville, op cit, p.59

33. Huntington, E.. The Historic Fluctuations of the Caspian Sea, Bulletin of the American Geographical Society, Vol 39, no. 10 1907, p.577-596

34. Gardner, Laurence, Realm of the Ring Lords, op cit, p.75

CHAPTER 13

1. Macbain, Alexander. Celtic Myth And Religion, A.& W. Mackenzie, Inverness, 1885, p.65

2. Holmes, T. Rice. Caesar's Conquest of Gaul, p.315 ref T.W. Rolleston. Myths and Legends of the Celtic Race, Thomas Cromwell, New York, 1911, p.19

3. Cited Comerford, T.. The History of Ireland, James Scanlan & B. Edes, Baltimore, 1826, p.14; Keating, Geoffrey. The History of Ireland, 1640. Although Keating's date of 800 BC is three thousand

years too late to be consistent with the monuments attributed to them.
4. Moore, Thomas. History of Ireland, Vol I, Baudry's European Library, Paris, 1837, p.60
5. Macbain, op cit
6. Leabhar na hUidhre, p.16
7. Kennedy, Patrick. The Bardic Stories of Ireland, McGlashan & Gill, Dublin, 1871, p.1-4
8. Cross, Teresa. Secrets of the Druids, Inner Traditions, Rochester, 2020, p.31
9. The Psalter of Cashel (the lost Book of Munster)
10. Chadwick, N.K. The Celts, Penguin, 1971
11. Ross, A.. Druids, Gods and Heroes from Celtic Mythology, Peter Lowe, 1986; and Hyde, D. A Literary History of Ireland, T. Fisher Unwin, 1899
12. Wilde, Lady. Ancient Legends, Mystic Charms & Superstitions of Ireland, Ward and Downey, London, 1887, p.256; Ohogain, Daithi. The Lore of Ireland: An Encyclopedia of Myth, Legend and Romance, The Collins Press, Dublin, 2006, p.48; Murphy, Andrew. Newgrange: Monument To Immortality, The Liffey Press, Dublin, 2012, p.160
13. Macbain, op cit, p.29
14. Burenhult, Goran. Stones and Bones: Formal disposal of the dead in Atlantic Europe during the Mesolithic-Neolithic interface 6000-3000 BC, British Archaeological Reports, 2004; Scarre, Christopher. Monuments and Landscape in Atlantic Europe: Perception and Society During the Neolithic and Early Bronze Age. Routledge, 2002, p. 145

15. Kador, Thomas, et al. Rites of Passage: Mortuary Practice, Population Dynamic, and Chronology at the Carrowkeel Passage Tomb Complex, Proceedings of the Prehistoric Society, doi:10.1017, 2018
16. Sykes, B.. Blood of the Isles, Corgi, London, 2006, p.190-91
17. Lebor Gabála Érenn (The Book of the Taking of Ireland)
18. Black, Jeremy, and Green, Anthony. Gods, Demons and Symbols of Ancient Mesopotamia: An Illustrated Dictionary, The British Museum Press, London, 1992, p.34
19. Cross, op cit, p.52
20. Gillies, H. Cameron. The Place Names of Argyll, David Nutt, London, 1906, p.3
21. O'Brien, Henry. Phoenician Ireland, Longman & Co, London, 1833, p.232
22. Teryan, Angela. Ancient Written Sources of European Nations About Their Ancestral Homeland: Armenia and Armenians, Voskan Yerevantsi, Yerevan, 2017, p.12-3
23. cited Kavoukjian, Martiros. Armenia, Subartu and Sumeria, Montreal, 1987, p.158-9
24. Quiggin, E., ed. Encyclopedia Britanica, 13, 1926; Teryan, op cit, p.15
25. Powell, T.G.E. The Celts, London, 1958, p.22
26. Kavoukjian, op cit, p.170
27. Budge, op cit
28. Coyne, Frank. An Upland Archaeological Study on Mount Brandon and The Paps, County Kerry. 2006. p.24
29. Monaghan, Patricia. The Encyclopedia of Celtic Mythology

and Folklore, Infobase Publishing, 2004, p.451

30. Armao, Frederic. Cathair Crobh Dearg: From Ancient Beliefs to the Rounds, University of Toulon, 2017, p.10

31. ibid, p.12

32. ibid

33. MacKillop, James. Dictionary of Celtic Mythology, Oxford University Press, 1998, p.110

34. Cross, op cit

35. Gray, L.H., ed. The Mythology of All Races, Vol. III, Marshall Jones Co., Boston, 1868, p.42-43

36. Oppenheimer, Stephen. The Origins of the British, Constable, London, 2006; McEvoy, B., et al. The Longue Durée of Genetic Ancestry: Multiple Genetic Marker Systems and Celtic Origins on the Atlantic Facade of Europe, American Journal of Human Genetics 75(4), 2004

37. Gardner, Realm of the Ring Lords, op cit, p.33

38. Baigent, M., Leigh, R., Lincoln, H.. Holy Blood, Holy Grail, Delacorte Press, New York, 1982, p.208-241

39. O'Grady, Standish. Silva Gadelica, London, 1892

40. Macbain, op cit, p.67

41. Graves, Robert. The White Goddess, Faber & Faber, London, 1961, p.64; Jubainville, H. D'Arbois de. The Irish Mythological Cycle, Albert Fontemoing, Paris, 1903, p.81-83

42. O'Grady, Standish. Early Bardic Literature, London, 1879, p.65

43. Gardner, op cit, p.31

44. ibid, p.33

45. Moore, op cit, p.62, citing O'Connor's Dissertations on the History of Ireland, and Collectan's Reflections on the History of Ireland, and Donald O'Neil in Fordun Scoti chronicles.

46. Gray, L.H., ed. The Mythology of All Races, Vol. III, Marshall Jones Co., Boston, 1868, p.45-46

47. Silva, Freddy. The Missing Lands, op cit, p.213-230

48. Black, Jeremy, op cit, p.34

49. Silva, op cit, p.218, 225

ADDITIONAL SOURCES

Brand, J.. A Brief Description of Orkney, Zetland, Pightland Firth, and Caithness, 1701

Cassidy, L, et al. A dynastic elite in monumental Neolithic society, Nature, 582, 384–388, 2020

Collins, G.H. The Geology of the Stones of Stenness, 1976

Contu, E. Il Nuraghe Santu Antine, Carlo Delfino editore, Sassari 1988

Cross, Teresa. Secrets of the Druids, Inner Traditions, Rochester, 2020

Dictionary of the Irish Language, Compact Edition, Royal Irish Academy, Dublin, Ireland, 1990

Elder, Isabel Hill. Celt, Druid and Culdee, Covenant Publishing Co., London 1973

Ellis, Peter Beresford. The Mammoth Book of Celtic Myths and Legends, Constable & Robinson, London, England, 2002

Galichian, Rouben. A Glance Into The History of Armenia, Bennett &

Bloom, London, 2015

Gerber, Pat. Stone Of Destiny, Canongate, Edinburgh, 1997

Higginbottom, Gail. The World Ends Here, the World Begins Here: Bronze Age Megalithic Monuments in Western Scotland, Journal of World Prehistory 2020, 33:25–134

Hnila, Pavol; Gilibert, Alessandra, et al. Prehistoric Sacred Landscapes in the High Mountains, Natur und Kult in Anatolien, BYZAS 24, 2019

Jamieson, John. Ancient Culdees of Iona, John Ballantyne and Co, Edinburgh, 1811

Jakobsen, Jakob, An Etymological Dictionary of the Norn Language in Shetland, Vilhelm Prior, Coenhagen, 1928

MacKillop, James. Dictionary of Celtic Mythology, Oxford University Press, New York,

Macalister, R. ed. And trans, Lebor Gabála Érenn: Book of the Taking of Ireland Part 1-5, Dublin: Irish Texts Society, 1941

Marwick, Ernest. An Orkney Anthology, Scottish Academic Press, Edinburgh, 1991

Melis, Paolo. Un approdo della costa di Castelsardo, fra età nuragica e romana, 2002. In, L'Africa romana: atti del 14, Convegno di studio, 7-10, Sassari, 2000

Mitri, Marco. An outline of the

Neolithic culture of the Khasi-Jaintia Hills of Meghalaya, India, John and Erica Hedges Ltd, Oxford, 2009

Michell, John. The New View Over Atlantis, Thames & Hudson, London, 1983

Monaghan, Patricia.Encyclopedia of Celtic Mythology and Folklore. Infobase Publishing, 2004

Moravetti, A. Ricerche archeologiche nel Marghine-Planargia. Il Marghine: monumenti: parte prima, Carlo Delfino Editore, Sassari, 1998

Movsisyan, Artak. The Writing Culture of Pre-Christian Armenia, Yerevan State University, Yerevan, 2006

Muir, T. The Mermaid Bride and Other Orkney Folk Tales, Kirkwall Press, Kirkwall, 1998

Parzinger, Hermann. Burial mounds of Scythian elites in the Eurasian steppe, Journal of British Academy, 5, 331-355, 2017

Petrosyan, A., and Bobokhyan, A., eds. The Vishap Stone Stelae, Academy of Sciences of Armenia, Gitutyun Publishing House Yerevan, 2015

Ponting, Margaret, and Gerald. Decoding the Callanish Complex. In Ruggles, Clive, and Whittle, A., eds., Astronomy and Society in Britain during the period 4000-1500 BC, BAR 88, Archaeopress,

Oxford, 1981

Rassu, M. Pozzi sacri: Architetture preistoriche per il culto delle acque in Sardegna, Condaghes, Cagliari, 2016

Richards, Colin. Dwelling Among The Monuments, McDonald Research Monograph, Cambridge, 2005

Ritchie, J. The Stones of Stenness, Proceedings of the Society of Antiquaries of Scotland, 1976

Robertson, J. D. M.. An Orkney Anthology: The Selected Works of Ernest Walker Marco Mitri, An outline of the Neolithic culture of the Khasi-Jaintia Hills of Meghalaya, India : an archaeological investigation, John and Erica Hedges Ltd. Oxford, 2009

Ross, A. Folklore of the Scottish Highlands, Tempus, Gloucester, 2000

Ruggles, Clive, and Barclay, Gordon. Cosmology, calendars and society in Neolithic Orkney, Antiquity, 74, 2000, p.62-74

Sanmark, Alexandra. Viking Law and Order, Edinburgh University Press, Edinburgh, 2017

Scarre, Chris. Neolithic Orkney in its European Context, MacDonald Research Monograph, Cambridge, 2000

Setyan, Vahan. Armenian Origins of

Basque, 2017

Sheridan, Alison. The Neolithic, Chalcolithic and Bronze Age in Argyll, Research Framework Symposium, Nov 2015

Storm, Gustav. Monumenta Historica Norwegie, 1882

Teryan, Angela. Ancient Written Sources of European Nations About Their Ancestral Homeland Armenia and Armenians, Voskan Yerevantsi, Yerevan, 2017

Ugas, Giovanni. L'alba dei Nuraghi , Fabula, Cagliari, 2006

Van Buren, Elizabeth, The Sign of the Dove, N. Spearman Publishing, London, England, 1983
Wainwright, F.T., The Northern Isles, Nelson, Edinburgh, 1962

Waite, A.E. The Hidden Church of the Holy Grail, 1909
Wallace, J.. A Description of the Isles of Orkney, W. Brown, 1693

Webster, Gary. A Prehistory of Sardinia 2300-500BC, Sheffield Academic Press, 1996

Webster, Gary. The Archaeology of Nuragic Sardinia, Equinox, 2015

West, J F (ed), The Journals of the Stanley Expedition to the Faroe Islands and Iceland in 1789, Vol I, Torshavn, 1970

Yacoubian, Adour. English-Armenian Dictionary, Shalom Pub, Brooklyn, 1993

IMAGE CREDITS

**Photos and maps by
Freddy Silva except:**

p.4 Rev Dr. Barry 1808; p.11
Johnathan Cleveley 1772; p.12
G. Barry 1805; p.14 Johnathan
Cleveley 1772; John Frederick
Miller, 1775; p.22 George Low
1772; p.30 George Petrie; F.L.W.
Thomas 1849; p.40 John Barber;
p.43,45, 46, 55 John Farrer 1862;
p.58, 59 after John Barber; p.81
James Kerr 1854; p.86 H. Sharbau
1860; p.91 F.L.W. Thomas 1860;
p.97 C.F. Cummings 1883;
p.109 Ordnance Survey 1907;
p.118 G. Cattermole 1833; p.122
Hydrographic Office 1860; p.138
Taramelli 1933; p.140 Giovanni
Lilliu 1938; p.146 Ulrico Hoeppi
1901, and F.L.W. Thomas 1860;
p.181 Kvaale, Creative Commons;
p.183 Thomas Pennant 1850;
p.184, 194, 195 Beiko, Creative
Commons; p.196 Rita Willaert,
Creative Commons; p.199 H.H.
Godwin-Austen 1876; p.219 Carlo
Bossoli 1856; p.220 J. Stuart
1867, MacLagan c.1850; p.238
William Wakeman c1895; p. 241
John Duncan; p.254 Constance
Frederica 1833

INDEX

OTHER WORKS by FREDDY SILVA

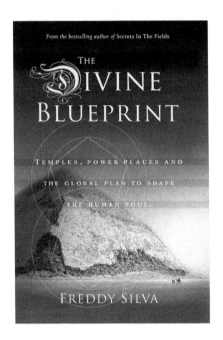

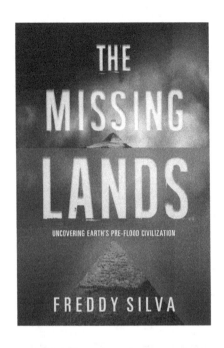

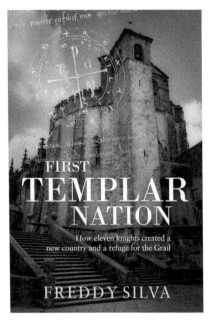

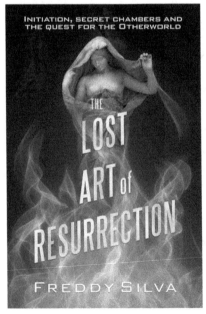

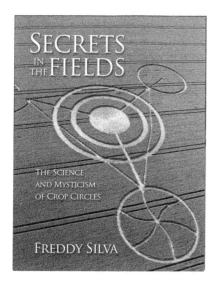

BOOKS AND DOCUMENTARIES

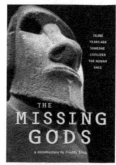

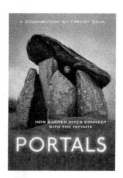

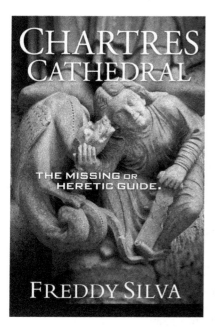

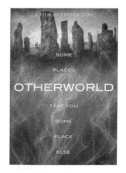

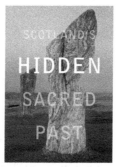

Available direct from the author at invisibletemple.com

Freddy Silva is a bestselling author, and one of the world's leading researchers of ancient civilizations and systems of knowledge, and the interaction between temples and consciousness. He has published seven books and over a dozen documentaries.

He is also a fine art photographer.

Described as "perhaps the best metaphysical speaker," he has lectured worldwide for two decades, with notable keynote presentations at the International Science and Consciousness Conference, and the International Society For The Study Of Subtle Energies & Energy Medicine, in addition to regular appearances on GAIA TV, podcasts and radio shows. He leads sell-out tours to sacred sites in England, Scotland, France, Portugal, Malta, Yucatan, Guatemala, Peru and Egypt.

When not living inside an airplane he can be found in England, New Zealand or America.

ancient wisdom for modern lives℠

www.invisibletemple.com